30
Steps to
Becoming
a Writer
and Getting Published

30
Steps to
Becoming
a Writer
and Getting Published

*The complete starter kit
for aspiring writers.*

Scott Edelstein

Writer's
Digest
Books

Cincinnati, Ohio

ACKNOWLEDGMENTS

The netline on page 44 originally appeared in *Surviving Freshman Composition* by Scott Edelstein (Lyle Stuart) and is copyright © 1990 by Scott Edelstein. It appears here by permission of the book's publisher, Carol Publishing Group.

"Loreen's Confession" by J.E. Sorrell originally appeared in *On the Other Side of the River* (Mid-List Press) and *In Broad Daylight* (The Mercury Publishing Company), and is copyright © 1990 by J.E. Sorrell. It appears here by permission of the author.

This hardcover edition of *30 Steps to Becoming a Writer—and Getting Published* features a "self-jacket" that eliminates the need for a separate dust jacket. It provides sturdy protection for your book while it saves paper, trees and energy.

Other fine Writer's Digest Books are available from your local bookstore or direct from the publisher.

02 01 00 99 98   8 7 6 5 4

Library of Congress Cataloging-in-Publication Data

Edelstein, Scott
   30 steps to becoming a writer—and getting published / by Scott Edelstein.
     p.   cm.
   Includes index.
   ISBN 0-89879-545-1
   1. Authorship. I. Title. II. Title: Thirty steps to becoming a writer.
PN153.E34   1993
808'.02—dc20   93-3675
                                                CIP

Edited by Jack Heffron
Designed by Brian Roeth

PART THREE

Getting Your Work Into Shape 72

PART FOUR

Getting More Experienced 98

PART FIVE

Getting Published 127

INTRODUCTION

How many times have you said to yourself, "I'd like to write" or "I wish I could become a writer"? How often have you dreamed of putting your ideas and feelings on paper—perhaps to be published and shared with others? And how many times have you met other writers, or read their work, and yearned to do what they do?

If the answer to any of the above questions is "More than once," this book is for you.

Plenty of people *want* to become writers, of course, and many of them want at least as much to get their work published. But many of them simply haven't known what to do to turn their dreams and desires into reality—or even how to get started in the first place. Perhaps you're in this situation yourself.

The problem is that, until now, no book has offered prospective writers a step-by-step program for attaining their goals and fulfilling their dreams.

Certainly there are plenty of writers' courses, conferences and workshops available, as well as several writers' magazines and literally hundreds of books on writing. Many of these can be quite useful. In fact, I've written several such books myself, including one for beginners: *The No-Experience-Necessary Writer's Course* (Scarborough House). But for all of their good advice and practical tips, none of these resources charts a clear, step-by-step course for becoming a writer.

30 Steps to Becoming a Writer—and Getting Published isn't like any of these other books and resources. It's based on a single essential premise: that you can learn to write moving and successful stories, essays, poems and other pieces by following a series of specific steps and instructions. Furthermore, you can use the same kind of step-by-step procedure to help get your work published in magazines, newspapers and other media.

It's possible to sing a beautiful ballad, knit an exquisite sweater, or grow a spectacular garden by following clear, careful, step-by-step instructions. Why should writing be any different? The answer, of course, is that it isn't. And it is just such a step-by-step approach that makes this book unique, practical, helpful and effective.

30 Steps to Becoming a Writer—and Getting Published offers you a consistent, well-planned program that starts with the basics, then takes you through a series of useful and inspiring steps, each designed to help you grow as a writer. By the time you've completed all thirty steps, you'll not only have finished several pieces of writing, you'll have submitted at least one of them to an editor for possible publication. Furthermore, you'll have become a practicing writer with some real experience, some completed works in your portfolio, and either some professional success or, at the very least, professional aspirations. Best of all, you'll have learned how to continue developing your writing skills on your own.

In short, you'll have attained your goal of becoming a writer. You'll do what, in the past, you only wished, dreamed or hoped you could do—someday.

And that's why I wrote this book: to help you turn your hopes and dreams into reality. Indeed, as you follow the steps in this book and get more and more words down on paper, you'll discover that your hopes and dreams are themselves often the source and material of good writing.

You don't need any special experience to follow this program. You don't need a college degree in English, or to be an avid reader of great literature (or anything else). You don't need to have taken courses in creative writing, and you don't need lots of writing experience under your belt. *All you need to get started is a desire to express yourself with words.*

Writing is and always will be a creative, intuitive, and sometimes mysterious process. Following a series of clearly defined steps doesn't change this reality a bit. Indeed, I can all but guarantee that some of what you write as you follow these steps will surprise (and often delight) you. You may discover things about yourself—what you know and feel and believe—that you didn't know before. That's wonderful. Each new insight can take you deeper into your own writing—and teach you more about yourself and the world.

No doubt you're wondering about my own background and experience as a writer. I started writing seriously as a teenager and have been doing it ever since, for twenty-five years now. I've published more than a hundred short stories and articles in magazines and anthologies around the world. I've also published more than a dozen books, including several specifically for writers. I've worked as a journalist, a literary agent, a writing and publishing consultant, a ghostwriter, a magazine columnist, an arts reviewer, a college-level writing teacher, and an editor for book, magazine and newspaper publishers. What's most important of all, though, is this: I love writing, and I enjoy helping others reach their own writing goals. I do this through one-on-one consultations, through my columns in writers' magazines, and through the books I've published on the art and craft of writing.

It's my hope that this particular book will help you to reach your own writing goals — and make your dream of becoming a writer come true.

One last word: If you know of someone else who has talked about wanting to become a writer but who hasn't managed to actually get started, please consider giving them this book as a gift (or loaning them your copy). You could be helping the next Mark Twain or Amy Tan launch their writing career.

Scott Edelstein
Minneapolis, Minnesota

PART ONE

Getting Started

Acquire the Basic Tools and Resources

One of the best things about writing is that it doesn't require any fancy or expensive equipment. For centuries writers have gotten by with nothing more than pens and paper. Despite all of the high-tech developments during the past decade, these two tools remain as reliable, useful and effective as ever. Indeed, many writers still do much or all of their writing in longhand, simply because it feels and works best for them.

The only tools you absolutely need to write, therefore, are paper and a pen or pencil. However, to get off to the best and most effective start, I suggest that you acquire the following:

- Several pens and/or pencils (your choice of style, point and color)
- A thick dictionary, preferably unabridged. Any large American dictionary will do. (I don't recommend the *Oxford English Dictionary*, since it follows British conventions and usage.)
- A thick thesaurus. This is a book that lists synonyms (words with similar or identical definitions). I recommend a thesaurus arranged alphabetically, rather than by subject.
- Erasers (both pencil and ink)
- Paper clips (regular and jumbo)
- Butterfly clamps (large paper clips shaped like butterflies, for holding large manuscripts together)
- Transparent tape
- Scissors
- Pencil sharpener
- File folders; a place to keep them (a cardboard box or milk crate will do); and a simple system for organizing them (e.g., alphabetically)

- Paper (your choice of size, style, color and thickness)
- Typing paper (white, unlined, 8½-by-11-inches, without holes) for manuscripts and business letters
- Plain white business (#10) envelopes
- Large (9-by-12-inches or 10-by-13-inches) envelopes, white or manila, for mailing manuscripts
- Blank mailing labels (about 1-by-3-inches)

The following are not strictly necessary, but they can be very useful:

- A good, sturdy stapler
- Staples
- Rubber bands
- A twelve-inch ruler
- A typewriter, word processor or computer with word processing software and a letter-quality printer
- Spare ribbons for your typewriter, word processor or printer
- Correction ribbons (if appropriate)
- Floppy disks (if appropriate)
- Correction tape (thin strips of adhesive white type—used for covering and correcting errors)
- Tax record book for keeping track of writing expenses and income

When it comes to writing implements, many writers have distinct preferences. I have a fondness for medium-point ballpoints with black ink. My wife, however, strongly prefers a fountain pen with blue ink and a delicate tip. One writer I've heard of uses half a dozen different-colored pens, each color signifying a different draft or purpose. Pick whatever feels right and looks best to you. Try different styles, points and ink colors until you find a combination that works well.

Also give some thought to the paper you'll write on. I have a strong preference for white unlined 8½-by-11-inch single sheets. Several writers I know, however, prefer lined legal pads. For many years, Natalie Goldberg, author of *Writing Down the Bones*, always used 8-by-10-inch spiral notebooks. Still other writers use bound blank books, usually 5-by-8-inches or 6-by-9-inches.

Although you can create your work on any kind of paper, final manuscripts and professional correspondence must be typed on 8½-by-11-inch unlined white paper, without holes. I recommend 20-lb.

photocopying or computer paper, which is available at office supply stores for two to four dollars per ream (five hundred sheets). You may also order paper and other office supplies, usually at still lower prices, from mail order office supply dealers such as Reliable (800-735-4000) and Viking (800-248-6111). Always prepare your final manuscripts on a typewriter (with a dark ribbon), word processor or (preferably) computer printer. Do not use a dot matrix printer, which is now considered substandard. Complete details on how to prepare a manuscript appear in Step 26.

You do not *absolutely* need to own a typewriter, computer or word processor to become a professional writer. Some writers produce their work in longhand, then pay a typist to prepare their final manuscripts. Nevertheless, I strongly recommend that you purchase a computer—not only for the ease it affords you in editing, correcting, rearranging, adding and deleting text, but because so many publishers now ask (or expect) to receive finished work on computer disk or via e-mail. Here are some tips on buying a computer (with the caveat that this page is being written in April of 1998 and thus will be out of date in the not-too-distant future):

• Prices on new computers drop so swiftly and steadily that what costs $1,500 new today will cost $1,000 new in six months and $600 new in a year. Your most cost-effective purchase is a new model that has been out for eight to twelve months and is about to be taken off the market. If you do some shopping around, the price on such a system will be the same as a used system with similar (or lesser) features.

• Either an IBM (or IBM clone) or Macintosh system is fine. However, Macs and Mac peripherals tend to cost about 25-35% more than IBM clones with similar features.

• Macs can automatically read (and save files to) most IBM disks. IBMs, however, cannot automatically work with Mac disks. For about $70 you can purchase a program for your PC which enables your IBM (or IBM clone) to use and save files to Macintosh disks. The best such program is MacDrive98.

• The best prices on computers and peripherals can usually be found at:

National retail stores: Office Max; Circuit City.

Catalogs: IBMs and IBM clones: PC Mall (800-555-MALL), MicroWarehouse (800-367-7080), PC Connection (800-800-5555); Damark (800-733-9070). Macs: Mac Connection (800-800-5555),

Mac Mall (800-222-2808); MacWarehouse (800-622-6222). Please note: many catalog companies can go lower than their published prices on many or most items. Once you know what you'd like to buy, ask the service representative what kind of room they have to play with in negotiating the price.

• If you buy an IBM or IBM clone, it should, at minimum, use Windows 95 or Windows 98 as its operating system; have at least 32 megabytes of RAM; run at a speed of at least 200 MHz; be upgradeable; and have either an Intel Pentium processor, a 686 processor from Cyrix or an AMD-K6 processor from AMD.

• There are now three standard word processing programs for writers: Microsoft Word, Microsoft Works, and ClarisWorks. I strongly recommend Microsoft Works, which is both inexpensive (about $70 for IBM, $100 for Mac) and versatile.

• 14″ color monitors now sell for as little as $150 for IBM, $250-$300 for Macs. Make sure the dot pitch is .28″ or smaller (anything larger provides inadequate resolution).

• Although ink-jet printers now sell for as little as $75, I strongly recommend a laser or LED printer. Laser printers are faster than ink jets, usually have higher resolution, last longer, and need repairs less often. New laser and LED printers sell for under $200 for IBMs, under $300 for Macs.

• Buy and install a good anti-virus program. Norton and IBM both make excellent anti-virus software. Cost: about $50.

• With some careful shopping, you should be able to buy a new, excellent, up-to-date, low-end system—complete with computer, CD-ROM drive, modem, color monitor, and laser printer—for $1,000 (IBM clone) or $1,400 (Mac).

YOUR ASSIGNMENT

Purchase (or otherwise acquire) everything on the list of basic items in this chapter. Also get any of the items in the "very useful" list that you feel will genuinely help you as a writer.

Once you have these items, you've completed Step 1. Now it's time for you to find and set up a regular place to write.

Set Up a Place to Work

J ust as you need to determine what basic writing equipment best suits you, it's important that you establish a place—or several places—where you can write comfortably and productively.

As you'd expect, different writers require different work environments. Some like to be surrounded by activity or sound; others prefer solitude and quiet. Jane Austen was able to write while family conversation went on all around her; Virginia Woolf, on the other hand, felt it essential to have a quiet, separate, private space set aside specifically for her writing.

Whatever your needs and preferences, the question to ask yourself is this: *What feels comfortable, yet helps me to remain alert and focused?*

For many writers, the answer is a coffee shop or restaurant, a library, or some other public place where they can sit and work—alone, yet in the midst of other people. For others, the ideal location might be a park bench, a rocking chair on the back porch, or the base of a favorite tree. The advent of laptop and notebook computers enables even those writers who are addicted to keyboards to work almost anywhere they choose.

Some writers need a distinctly private space where they can control the level of noise and activity. For these people, a spot that is all their own, at least for certain scheduled hours, is essential. This doesn't necessarily have to be a separate room. Often a corner of the dining room or bedroom will do.

Still other writers have two, three or even more places where they write, depending on their mood, their needs, and the circumstances of the moment.

Whatever location you choose, be sure that you arrange it to *your* liking. Some basics to consider include lighting, temperature, ventilation, back support (can you write for extended periods without feeling stiff?), and the proper height and angles for your writing arm (or, if you use a keyboard, for your hands and wrists). Remember that what works best for someone else may not work for you. (Mark Twain did much of his writing lying in bed; I've tried it a few times, and each time I fell quickly asleep.)

If you need or prefer quiet, try to find a place to work where you can shut the door and windows. If this simply isn't possible, wear ear plugs. Consider unplugging your phone while you work, or moving it to another room, or hooking up an answering machine.

If you're like many writers, you may actually prefer to have music, or even news or talk shows, playing in the background as you write. If you fit this profile, have the appropriate equipment set up and ready to use, and keep a selection of tapes, CDs or records nearby.

If you need or prefer privacy, being able to close (and perhaps lock) your door is essential, particularly if you have kids. Or, set up your work space in a part of your home where people rarely go, such as the attic or garage. Another option is to rent a room or other space outside of your home. If none of these arrangements is possible, try setting your work space apart with an Oriental-style folding screen.

No matter what your physical setup, you can only have privacy if other people let you alone. Make a clear agreement with other members of your household that at certain times you are not to be disturbed, except in genuine emergencies. If anyone violates that agreement, shoo them out promptly and firmly, and insist that they honor the privacy agreement in the future.

Thus far I've discussed practical considerations; now let's turn to some aesthetic ones.

If possible, find or arrange a spot that has a pleasant view (but not so pleasant that it distracts you from writing). If you can, decorate your work space so that it's inviting and inspiring. Keep a pot of coffee, or a cooler of soft drinks, or a jar full of pretzels nearby. Type up some inspiring quotations and tape them to the wall next to you or on the front cover of the notebook you write in.

Your work space should of course be functional as well as comfortable. Keep important files, extra paper, pens and other supplies where they can be easily reached. Keep everything well organized, so that you can quickly find whatever you need.

If you write in more than one place, make one spot your "home base." This might be the place where you do most of your writing, or it may simply be the spot where you keep all of your supplies and writing-related files.

The same principles of comfort and functionality apply to how you dress when you write. Wear what feels good, keeps you sufficiently warm or cool, and doesn't restrict the movement of your arms, hands or fingers. In the winter I do much of my writing in my bathrobe; in the summer I often wear nothing but a pair of swimming trunks.

In addition to setting up your work space, you may want to establish a regular prewriting ritual. I don't mean something religious or spiritual (though you can include these elements if you like), but a quick routine that gets you in the mood to write. For example, you might begin each writing session by getting a cup of coffee and whistling for your dog; or you might sharpen a pencil and reread the previous day's work; or you might put on your favorite slippers, do fifty jumping jacks, and select a CD to listen to while you write.

Whatever ritual you devise, be sure that it takes no more than ten minutes. Remember, its purpose is to warm you up and get you in the mood to write, not to help you put off getting started.

Is a prewriting ritual necessary for every writer? Not really. If you can get yourself in the right frame of mind by simply sitting down and picking up your pen—or turning on your computer—those two actions can serve as the only prewriting ritual you will need.

YOUR ASSIGNMENT

Find one or more places where you can write comfortably and productively. If you locate more than one, designate one as your home base.

Prepare each writing site to be as pleasant and functional as possible. Pay attention to posture and position, seating, temperature, privacy, noise level and other essential details. Then, unless you'll be writing in a public place, add some personal extras—photographs, flowers, posters, a tea kettle, a portable CD player, inspiring quotations, etc.—to make your work space still more comfortable and attractive.

Set up your desk or other writing surface, and arrange all the supplies and materials you need close at hand.

Finally, if you like, devise a prewriting ritual that helps you to make a smooth and effective transition from your everyday life to the concentrated attention of writing.

Now step back and admire your work space.

Congratulations on completing Step 2. You've laid the groundwork for productive and successful writing by establishing a spot that's yours and yours alone — one that's designed to nurture your writing.

Step Three

Begin a Writer's Notebook

writer's notebook is a place to record your ideas, observations, anecdotes, images, outlines, descriptions, notes and other raw material for your writing. Although most writers keep a notebook of some sort, there are probably as many different ways to keep one as there are writers alive on the planet. In Steps 4-7, as well as in many of the later steps, we'll explore some of the ways in which your notebook can be used.

A writer's notebook is different from a journal or diary, where you record your thoughts, feelings and concerns. A journal is a strictly personal undertaking, a volume about yourself that you keep for yourself. In contrast, a writer's notebook exists to *support your writing*, and to provide material and inspiration for it.

I don't mean to suggest that you shouldn't keep a journal; in fact, many writers regularly write in both a notebook and a journal. If you like, you can even merge your notebook and journal into a single ongoing record – so long as you don't neglect the purposes of a writer's notebook described above.

Some writers organize their notebooks chronologically, as in a diary. Others divide up their notebooks according to subject. For instance, you might break up your notebook into sections pertaining to the different pieces you're working on – e.g., Ghost Poem, Kidnapping Story, Highway Editorial, Book Proposal, etc. Or, if you're a fiction writer, you might separate your notebook into a variety of sections titled Characters, Images, Story Ideas, Dialogue, Places/Settings and so on.

Some writers don't just write down useful and important items in their notebooks, but actually draft most of their pieces in them as well. This is fine. (These writers usually fill up notebooks very quickly, perhaps one every few months.)

Actually, the term *writer's notebook* can be a bit misleading. You don't have to go out and buy a spiral notebook or three-ring binder. A bound blank book, a legal pad, a set of file folders, a box of loose pages, or a computer disk will all do. The benefit of an actual notebook, however, is that you can carry it with you wherever you go, so it's always available to make notes in whenever something strikes you.

On the other hand, maybe you don't want the burden of always carrying a book around. Or perhaps, like me, you want to keep your notebook in your work space at all times so that it can't be lost or misplaced. If either of these is the case, simply carry a pen and a blank sheet of paper with you. When a thought, observation or incident strikes you as significant, write it down on the blank paper; then, when you get back to your desk, transfer it into your notebook.

YOUR ASSIGNMENT

Think for a few minutes about what sort of writer's notebook will work best for you: a spiral notebook; a blank bound book; a three-ring binder; a legal pad; a set of folders, organized according to dates or topics; computer files; or some other system that I haven't mentioned. Then pick (or design) the one that feels most appropriate.

Exactly how you choose to organize your notebook is up to you, so long as your method is both functional and comfortable. Whatever arrangement you decide on, however, should be one that lets you add, review and locate material easily and quickly.

Once you've made your decision, buy whatever items you need. Put your name, address and phone number(s) on your notebook, as protection in case you misplace it. Then divide your notebook into sections and write in appropriate headings. If at some later point you wish to organize your notebook in a different manner, that's of course fine.

Now your writer's notebook is ready—and you're ready to begin writing. You'll use your notebook to complete Steps 4-7—and to support and inform your writing for many years to come.

Step Four

Determine and Record Your Goals

O ne of the first things you can use your notebook for is recording your writing goals.

Setting realistic goals can help you to get started writing — and, once you've started, they can help you to keep on writing, week after week and month after month, as your skills steadily develop. Then, after you've reached each goal, you can look back and appreciate how far you've come, how much you've achieved, and how well your efforts have paid off.

Even if you don't succeed in reaching a goal, setting it will still have proven useful, because it will have encouraged you to put forth serious and sustained effort.

Setting reasonable goals isn't always easy, however. It's tempting to start with highly ambitious goals — but the more ambitious they are, the easier it is to fall short of them or grow discouraged. Remember, you're setting writing goals entirely for your own benefit — so set attainable ones.

Any goal that you set for your writing should reflect your own efforts rather than the judgments and decisions of others. Having a poem accepted for publication by a literary magazine within a year may sound like a reasonable goal at first, but it's based on the decisions of editors, who can be quirky and capricious. A better goal for your first year as a writer might be to write several poems *worthy* of publication by literary magazines, and to submit those poems to the editors of at least three such magazines. This goal is based solely on your own efforts and ability, not on what others do.

Your writing goals should be specific and concrete — for example, "to complete three short opinion pieces on education" or "to spend two hours a day, four days a week writing essays on education." "To write up my ideas on education," while a perfectly legitimate intention, is too amorphous to serve as a useful goal.

The most effective goals are those that are tough enough to make you stretch, and maybe even sweat, but not so distant or difficult that you want to give up in frustration.

Here are some examples of clear, effective, realistic writing goals. You may wish to adopt one or more of them for your first year as a writer:

- To write for at least two hours a week, and to see where this takes you
- To write at least three short stories that you're reasonably happy with
- To keep a writer's notebook for a minimum of six months, and to use material from that notebook to create several finished pieces
- To write at least one essay every two months, and, after ten months, to submit the three best essays to magazines or newspapers for publication
- To write for an hour a day, four days a week, and to try your hand at writing poetry, fiction, prose poems and essays
- To go through *30 Steps to Becoming a Writer — and Getting Published* from beginning to end, completing every one of the thirty steps

What if you're not a goal-oriented person — or if you're not even sure whether writing is something you'll want to keep doing? Then set the following three goals for yourself:

- To write on a regular basis for six months (or some other length of time)
- After six months, to examine your strengths and weaknesses as a writer and to evaluate what you've written
- To decide where to go and what to do next with your writing

Many writers do their best and most productive work when they follow a regular writing schedule. One of your goals, therefore, may be to stick to a writing schedule of your own design.

A schedule can keep you focused and on track, and it can help you establish a useful writing routine. Beginners in particular often need the extra dose of motivation that a schedule can provide. Furthermore, a schedule enables you to declare to others that during certain hours you cannot be disturbed. And if you're a busy person who must plan your leisure time in advance, a writing schedule is absolutely essential.

Other writers, however, respond better to the rhythms of their own bodies and psyches than they do to those of the clock. If this description fits you, or if your life is simply too unpredictable to allow you to schedule specific writing times, set a goal to write for a certain *amount* of time each week, but don't commit yourself to a specific schedule. An example: "I'll write three to five hours each week."

If you're not sure whether you'll do better with or without a formal schedule, try both options. You should discover quickly which works best for you.

YOUR ASSIGNMENT

Get out your writer's notebook and find a group of three or more blank pages. At the top of these pages, write the following:

Page 1   *Why I Want to Write*
Page 2   *Things That Intrigue Me About Writing*
Page 3   *Writing Goals for the Next Year*

Start with page one. On this page, make a list of all of the reasons why you're interested in writing. Don't censor yourself. It doesn't matter whether a reason is selfish or noble, significant or trivial, realistic or pure fantasy. If it's a genuine reason, write it down. Some examples: "To change the world"; "to become wealthy and famous"; "to amuse myself"; "for ego gratification"; "to communicate my feelings and ideas to others"; "for catharsis"; "to convince others of certain ideas and beliefs"; "to create great, lasting art"; "to prove to myself that I can write as well as my sister"; "to play with words"; "to find an enjoyable way to make a living on my own"; "to write my grandparents' life story"; "to get more in touch with my feelings"; "to feel more comfortable writing letters, memos, reports and other everyday items"; "to impress my parents"; "to earn an extra $10,000 or more per year"; "to see my name in print"; "to have a regular outlet for my fantasies"; "to be able to preserve important memories for my children and grandchildren"; "to experiment with form and meter"; "as a fun and entertaining hobby."

When you've finished this list, turn to page two. Think about the things that intrigue or interest you about writing, and write them down. Again, don't censor yourself. Some examples: "The way words can engender emotions in people"; "prose poems"; "imagery"; "presenting people's thoughts in prose, as an internal monologue";

"creating a vivid sense of place"; "twisting reality to make it more moving and exciting"; "making strange or surreal connections"; "choosing just the right details to make something come alive."

Once you've finished this second list, stop writing. Then spend a few minutes looking over both lists carefully, and ask yourself what each list tells you about who you are and what you want to get out of writing.

Now you're ready for page three. Using the items in the first two lists as raw material, come up with three to five specific, concrete and realistic goals that you hope to reach through your writing *within the next year*. If you like, look back at the examples of goals that appear earlier in this step.

If you come up with more than five goals, write them all down; then look them over carefully, pick the five that mean the most to you, and cross out the others. (You may want to set some of these other goals later, after you have more writing experience under your belt.)

Don't look beyond the first year right now. If a goal means a lot to you but will require more than a year to reach, write it on a separate page and save it for the future.

If setting goals for your first year of writing seems too long range, it's okay to use a shorter period of time – say, six, eight or ten months.

Once you've written your list of goals, look them over carefully. Do they genuinely cover the things that are most important to you right now? Given your current level of available time, energy and interest, are they truly attainable? Is anything about your goals missing, vague or less than accurate? Make changes or additions as necessary.

Next, put a date at the top of this third list, so that you'll be able to look back and see how far you've come, and how long (or short) a time it took you to get there.

Finally, post this list in your work space, in a spot where you will see it every time you sit down to write. Or, if you prefer, tape your list on the outside cover of your writer's notebook. From now on, each time you sit down to write, first review the list for a few seconds.

Now you're done with Step 4 – and you've completed your first writing assignment. You've discovered a large number of things that are important to you – and you've written them down. *You've succeeded in putting words onto paper in a meaningful way.*

As the year goes by, keep track of your progress as you come closer to achieving your goals. And keep in mind that *you're* the one who set those goals—which means that you always have the right to change them. In fact, writing goals often change over time as a writer gains writing experience and grows more in tune with their own strengths and desires.

Now let's move from setting goals to discovering your own natural material for your writing.

Note Your Interests, Enthusiasms and Passions

One of the big questions on your mind may be, "Where do writers get their material?" Or, to put it more personally, "Where will I find mine?"

The answer is that writers find good material *every-where*: in their memories, experiences, observations, reading, thinking, fantasizing, obsessing—and simply in being alive and aware.

Perhaps a more important question is, "How do writers sort through everything they experience, feel and imagine, in order to decide what's important and what's not?" In other words, how do writers determine what's meaningful to them? And how can you discover what's meaningful to you?

The answer to this last question is that you already know what's meaningful to you—you just may not have taken the time to spell it out. Something is meaningful to you if it generates strong feelings inside of you, or if it makes you stop and pay attention to it, or if you find yourself spending a lot of time doing it, observing it or thinking about it. If something excites you, scares you, saddens you, delights you, worries you, comforts you, angers you or satisfies you, it has meaning for you—even if you can't express exactly what that meaning is.

Literally thousands of things hold meaning for you. Some of them—your family, a warm fire on a winter night, the smell of fresh-baked bread, the long illness of a friend—will feel important for reasons you can easily explain and understand. Others—the sight of a jogger straining up a hill, an old stone water tower squatting in front of bare winter trees, the smell of gasoline, the sway of a moving subway car—might not be so easy to explain. As you observe your own life—your own thoughts, actions and reactions—you'll find that many things evoke strong feelings in you. These items are your own natural material, the things for you to use in your writing.

The best way to write well is to write about what you care about — the things you love, like, hate, fear, worry about, obsess over, yearn for, avoid, can't accept, can't comprehend, or can't come to terms with. The more you work with these, the more you'll move your readers.

You don't have to know how or why something is meaningful to you in order to use it in your writing. Good writing doesn't have to analyze or explain things (though there's nothing inherently wrong with analysis or explanation, either). However, good writing *does* move and convince readers, by making them care about the same things you care about.

YOUR ASSIGNMENT

Get out your writer's notebook that you began in Step 3. Turn to a blank page. Make sure several more blank pages follow.

Sit quietly and comfortably for two or three minutes, doing nothing more than following your breath as it goes in and out of your body. Then, slowly, turn your attention to those people, ideas, sensations, items, images, events and actions that somehow have meaning for you. As each item occurs to you, write it down.

Keep your descriptions simple; each item should be no longer than ten or twelve words (e.g., "the night we spent at the Hagens' and ate midnight popovers" or "an old woman sledding, laughing with delight"). Don't write whole sentences or paragraphs, or elaborate descriptions — you can always write these later if you like. Often one or two words (e.g., "rabbit fur," "math anxiety" or "infidelity") will be sufficient.

Be as specific as possible. "The way a mother smiles at her child" is fine, but "The way Maria smiled at Rose as she fed the ducks at Lake Nokomis" is better still, because it refers to a specific memory. "Coney Island" is good, but "the smell of electricity, cooking oil and sugar at Coney Island" is stronger and sharper.

You may find that one item on your list generates half a dozen others. Thus, "Coney Island" might prompt you to write down a series of items: "Louisa grabbing the brass ring and falling off the carousel," "kissing Clark on the beach," "mating sand crabs," "my first Nathan's hot dog," "the Parachute Jump," and "getting lost at night at age seven and taking the subway home alone." Another example: "Justice" might lead to "Thurgood Marshall in the 1960s," "getting punished for what Mark did to Julie," "Jefferson's slaves," "the signs outside Sandstone Prison," "ethics vs. needs," and "Karla's arrest and trial."

Again, don't censor yourself. No one will read your list except you—unless, of course, you invite them to. Don't be afraid to record your obsessions, your irrational fears, your sexual fetishes or fantasies, or any disturbing images that may appear. Whatever comes, let it come; you may be able to use it in your writing, either as is or altered. In fact, some of those images that disturb or frighten you may result in some of your most gripping and powerful writing, precisely *because* they disturb or frighten you. (Many writers, including Edgar Allan Poe, created some of their best work by drawing on their fantasies and fears.) Of course, if you choose later not to work with any of the items that disturb you, that's fine. But write them down for the moment, so you don't lose or forget them.

If you have trouble getting started, begin your list with these four items, which just about everyone cares about: *sex, sleep, food* and *death*. See if you can list some specific images, events or concerns for each of the four. Once you've done that, continue adding new items of your own.

Go as quickly or as slowly as you need to. If you need to search your mind and heart carefully, that's fine. If the items come pouring out on their own, that's fine, too.

Continue compiling this list, filling up as many pages as you need to, until you feel yourself naturally begin to wind down. Then keep going for a few minutes more, and stop. Most people finish up after about half an hour; but if you're still going strong at the end of half an hour, keep writing—but for no more than an hour in all.

When you've finished, look over your list—which will probably run several pages—from beginning to end. It will almost certainly include a diverse range of subjects and emotions. Some of the items on the list will be people, things and events that have stuck with you for years; others may seem to come completely out of the blue. Some may be things you forgot for years and suddenly remembered again. Any of these items, however, may eventually prove useful to your writing.

If additional ideas or images come to you as you read your list— and they probably will—write these down as well.

Now put your list away for a while—a few hours, a day, or even a week or two. Then come back to your favorite writing spot, prepare yourself with plenty of blank pages, and get ready to repeat the process—but this time with a difference.

As before, relax and get comfortable. Also as before, follow your breath in and out for a while. This time, though, do it for ten minutes instead of just two or three. If your mind wanders—and it probably will—gently bring it back to your breathing again.

When ten minutes have elapsed, begin writing. This time, though, instead of consciously searching your memory and heart for the things that move you, *don't search for anything at all*. Instead, simply let your mind wander. Don't try to control or direct it.

Things will pop into your consciousness, stay there for a time, and then disappear again, to be replaced by other thoughts and images. Some will be mundane, others fraught with meaning. Some will surprise or shock you; others will please or excite or delight you. Whenever something moving or meaningful appears, write it down.

Continue this process for half an hour, then stop.

Look through your second list carefully, adding any new items that may come to mind as you review it. Then compare it to the list you wrote earlier. Which list is longer? Which contains the items that you find the most moving and meaningful? Which list intrigues or inspires you more?

If the first list has more or better material, you probably work best by deliberately searching among your concerns, ideas, images and memories. If your second list seems stronger, you probably work better intuitively, using a less deliberate process of letting your mind wander at will.

Save both of your lists indefinitely. They will serve as source material for your writing for weeks, months or even years to come. Whenever you're unsure what to write next—or when you're stuck for the right line, image, idea, character, event or plot twist—simply look over your list again. Chances are good that you'll find what you need somewhere on that list.

Add to this list whenever an idea, an event, an image or an important memory occurs to you. In fact, you might want to spend fifteen to thirty minutes a week repeating either or both parts of this step. You can do this week after week, year after year. Or, if you prefer, you can do it whenever the time feels right, or when you've used up most of the items on your existing list—or whenever you feel your writing needs a jolt of new energy and inspiration. This process will provide you with a never-ending source of ideas and images to work from — a huge vein of material to mine.

Now look back at what you've accomplished in this step. You've answered *for yourself* the question, "Where do I get material for my writing?" Not only that, you've found an answer that will work for you for as long as you continue writing. Furthermore, you've discovered a source of material — your own memories, feelings, images, concerns and ideas — that will constantly replenish itself year after year.

And now for the best news of all: This list will serve as only one of three different sources of material for your writing, each one rich with detail and meaning, and each one constantly growing. In Steps 6 and 7 I'll introduce you to these other two sources, and you'll discover how to develop both of them to benefit your writing.

Record Your Observations

Now you know how to reach into your heart, your mind and your memories for material that moves and affects you. In this step, you'll have the chance to explore a different, but equally inexhaustible, source of material: your day-by-day experience.

Each of us, no matter who we are, has an enormous wealth of daily experience to draw from. What we live through, encounter and observe can continually provide us with useful insights, ideas and images. We need only learn to direct our full attention to each moment as we live it.

This is as true for the homemaker who has never left rural Indiana as it is for the internationally famous actor who has traveled the world. While some of us have a wider variety of experiences than others, all of us share the same fundamental human feelings, problems and concerns. We all have desires, dreams, needs, fears, disappointments and worries. We have all experienced joy, loss, loneliness, shock, delight, despair, and a multitude of other feelings. Internally, your life is fundamentally no different from the lives of every other human being on the planet; only the external particulars differ. This is why a factory worker in Denver can enjoy reading a story about a fisherman from Taiwan, a poem about a philosopher from Venice, a play about a Russian thief, or an essay about Peruvian farmers—and it is why others can appreciate and empathize with your experience, regardless of how expansive or limited it may be.

Often, however, we fail to appreciate just how full, profound and vivid our own lives can be. Instead of fully engaging ourselves in each moment as it appears before us, we separate ourselves from it and hold parts of ourselves back. Our habit is to focus only a small part of our attention on what happens around us—just enough to conceive and categorize things ("a cloudy sky," "a huge oak desk," "an angry, tired clerk"). The rest of our attention gets set aside, to think, evaluate, or be concerned with other things. We don't participate in the fullness of the moment.

Yet if we were to truly focus our attention on any one person, object or event — even for a few seconds — we would frequently find it rich with detail, significance and meaning. We would discover that much of our "mundane" existence is, in fact, abundant, expressive and often surprising.

In short, if you are alert and observant, every moment of your life is a moment that may provide material for your writing. All you must do is pick those incidents, observations and ideas that are most significant and most worth relating to others.

"Aha!" you say. "But how do I know what in my daily experience is significant and what's not?"

You know in the same way that you knew in Step 5 what was meaningful for you. If something moves you in some way — if it delights you, disturbs you, shocks you, angers you, pleases you, confuses you, haunts you, panics you, or simply sticks with you over time — it has real significance for you.

And what should you do when you experience something meaningful? *Write it down in your notebook.*

YOUR ASSIGNMENT

Completing this step involves three short assignments.

1. Find a building you've never been inside of before. This can be an office building, a warehouse, a home, an aircraft hangar, a hotel, an abandoned factory — any building that intrigues you. Locate a room in this building where you can be completely alone for fifteen minutes.

Enter the room and, if possible, close the door behind you. Scan the entire room slowly and carefully, including the ceiling and floor. Take note of the colors, textures, designs and angles. Notice the different materials used to construct the walls, the floor, the windows and the ceiling. Observe any details that might not be visible at first — sprinkler heads, moldings, graffiti, broken window latches, chipped paint, etc. Then take a walk around the room, observing it from different angles. Look for new details with each step.

As you walk, run your hand along various surfaces, noting their textures, temperatures, angles, etc. Also pay attention to how the floor feels beneath your feet.

When you've walked completely around the room, stop and stand still. For a minute or two, listen to all of the sounds in the room — e.g., the whoosh of air blowing through heating vents, the dull throb of machinery, the creak of old beams in the wind, the rattle of a loose window, voices drifting in from outside, or the sound of your own breathing.

Now focus your attention on the air in the room. Is it dry or moist? Warm or cool? Does it smell fresh, musty, salty, greasy, disinfected? Are other smells wafting in from outside?

Next, examine some of the objects in the room. Pick the half dozen that seem most interesting to you. One by one, pick them up or run your hands over them. Turn them over — or kneel down — and examine them from unusual angles. Hold them against your cheek, your elbow, or the back of your knee. Put your nose up against each of them and inhale deeply. If you like, and it's not potentially harmful, taste them briefly with your tongue.

Finally, look at the entire room from two or three unusual angles. Lie down on the floor, first on your back, then on your stomach; stand on a desk or table and look down; find some other unusual perspective. Spend about half a minute observing the room from each of these vantage points. Then leave the room.

Once you're outside, review some of the most striking or unusual details you noticed about the room. What surprised you? What did you find out that you hadn't known or thought about before? What about the room affected or intrigued you? Write down these items in your notebook.

In doing this first assignment, you've taught yourself to carefully observe, to look for details that might not be immediately apparent, and to view the same setting, object or event from a variety of angles. You can use this technique, which I call *close observation*, anywhere and at any time. You can use it over and over — not just for settings and places, but for objects, people, concepts, actions, incidents, and entire sequences of events.

This technique will often yield insights, connections and meanings that you might ordinarily have overlooked. And the more you practice close observation, the easier it will get, the better you will get at it, and the more natural it will seem.

In the future, whenever something catches your attention or

strikes you as important, intriguing or worth noticing, stop what you're doing for a short time and switch into close observation mode. For a minute or two — or, if your time is limited, for a few attentive seconds — focus your full attention on that object, person, setting or event, taking note of all the details, nuances and complexities that you can. Then, as soon as possible, write down what you observed that feels significant or important. Sometimes this may mean writing down all of your observations, item by item and detail by detail. At other times, it may be enough to jot down only a few key words, such as "Martina's attic," if these will be sufficient to bring a complete, detailed memory to life for you.

If you don't have time to write down all of your close observations immediately, jot down the key items as notes; then, as soon as possible — but certainly within twenty-four hours — come back to your notebook, reread those notes, and write out everything in as much detail as necessary.

With practice, you'll soon be able to engage in close observation at a moment's notice, whenever you wish, or whenever something moves or intrigues you.

2. Go to some public place where you feel comfortable — a park, a coffee shop, a hotel lobby — at a time when there will be lots of people around. Bring your notebook and a couple of pens or pencils. Find a spot near the center of the action, get comfortable, and open your notebook on your lap.

For the next forty-five to sixty minutes, deliberately eavesdrop on the conversations of the people near you, including those who walk past. Focus your attention not only on what each person says, but on the inflections, accents and emotions in their voices as well. Note how each person is dressed, how they hold themselves, how they gesture, how they smell and so on. Write down anything that intrigues, amuses, moves or inspires you.

Be discreet in all your observations, of course. Don't give people any clues that you're listening in; in fact, to preserve your anonymity and safety, it's best to look in a different direction most of the time.

Later, when you get back to your work space, look over what you've written. If anything in your notes leads to more ideas, images or connections, write these down as well.

Once you've done this, you've learned yet another useful, important and deceptively simple technique for finding and developing material for your writing. You've learned how to draw from *others'* experience as well as your own. Furthermore, by actively listening to what others say and letting it spark ideas, images and connections of your own, you've combined your experience with theirs. You can use this technique of drawing fresh material from other people's lives any time you wish.

3. Put your notebook and a couple of pens or pencils next to your bed before you go to sleep. The next morning, as soon as you awaken, open the notebook and spend ten minutes reviewing your dreams from the night before, as well as any ideas and insights you may have had while falling asleep or waking up. Write down anything that seems significant or meaningful.

Carry your notebook with you throughout the day, jotting down notes whenever something catches your attention or moves you. Then, toward the end of your day—sometime between supper and sleep—take about twenty minutes to review and reflect on the events of the day. Write down whatever insights, ideas and observations come to you.

This simple practice of making regular notes and doing a daily review of your experience can result in a wealth of rich and important material. Try it for one day; then use it again as often as you wish. If you like, make it part of your standard daily activities.

You've accomplished a great deal in Step 6. You've learned several techniques for observing the world more closely, for recording those observations, and for turning close observation into a habit. Most important, you've gotten some hands-on experience in using your daily life as a source of material for your writing.

Now you're ready to begin tying some of this material together.

Put Your Thoughts and Ideas on Paper

S o far you've discovered two abundant and easily accessible sources of material for your writing: your own past — your memories, thoughts and feelings — and your current experiences and observations. In this step you'll explore a third wellspring of material: your ability to make connections, associations and logical and intuitive leaps. You'll deliberately create something new out of the material you've accumulated from other sources.

Each of us constantly analyzes, synthesizes and evaluates the information that flows into our minds and hearts. We do this to create an internal picture of the universe in which we live. Each of us tries to form as accurate a picture as possible; nevertheless, each person's internal picture is always unique.

This process takes place both consciously and unconsciously. Your conscious mind weighs evidence, sifts through information and comes to conclusions; your unconscious speaks to you through feelings, hunches, dreams and intuition. Both parts of this process, however, have a single central focus: *What is most important, meaningful or intriguing to you?* What interests you, fascinates you, or moves you? The more closely you pay attention to these questions, the more vivid and telling your writing is likely to be, the more likely it is to move and convince others, and the more satisfaction and pleasure you are likely to gain from creating it. In short, the more you remain true to your own cares, concerns and impulses, the more your readers will be able to empathize with you, understand you, and appreciate what you have to say.

YOUR ASSIGNMENT

This step, like the previous one, includes three brief assignments.

1. Take out your writer's notebook, a pen or pencil, and several

blank sheets of paper. These should be loose pages, so you don't have to keep flipping back and forth in your notebook.

Slowly and carefully, look over all of the notes you have made thus far in response to the assignments in Steps 4, 5 and 6 — as well as any additional notes you may have made on your own. As you look through all of these notes, do several things:

First, look for any ideas, images, themes, people, settings or even specific words that appear repeatedly. For instance, you may find that *scenes* — from childhood, past winters, Germany or baseball games — occur often in your notes. Or perhaps food, or jazz, or wild animals, or solitude, or danger, or fear of aging appears as a recurrent *theme*. Maybe there is a common *viewpoint* — the outsider looking in, the seeker hoping to make sense of events, or the discontented critic hoping to change things for the better. Or perhaps what surfaces is a particular kind of *relationship*: the relationship of individuals to government, of emotional expression to spiritual development, of psychology to education, or of adolescence to middle age. Or maybe you see a unity of certain *images*: images of poverty, light, sudden change, aimless movement, the large enveloping the small.

Whatever connections and patterns emerge, write them down. But don't simply note those connections; write down what they mean to you, as well as any thoughts, images or incidents that those associations lead you to. Don't hold back or censor yourself; write it all down, using as many words and pages as you need. If one thing leads to another, and then to another, and then to yet another, that's wonderful. If, by the time you're done, you've completed a draft (or a large part of a draft) of a story, poem or essay, that's better still.

As you do all this, observe your own reactions. What do you respond to most strongly, enthusiastically or anxiously? Highlight each of these items in some way — by underlining it, or circling it, or placing a star before it. Each of these items can likely become the basis for a poem, story, essay, or other piece of writing.

2. Now that you've become familiar not only with the things you care about, but with some of the relationships among them, you're ready to take the process a step further.

Look again at what you've written on the loose sheets of paper, as well as at any highlighted (underlined, starred, etc.) items in your notebook. (If you've got lots of items to choose from, feel free to limit yourself to the five or six that most attract you.) For each of these items, ask yourself the following questions:

- What most interests, intrigues, fascinates or moves me about this?
- What would I most like to do with it?
- What do I most want to say about it?
- What would I most like to see happen with it or to it?
- What would I most like to read about it?

Take as much time as you wish to answer these questions for each of the items described above. On more of your loose pages, write down your answers to each question. Again, don't limit or censor yourself, or force yourself to stick to what may seem reasonable, appropriate or socially acceptable.

As you answer these questions, all sorts of concepts, images and events — perhaps even entire paragraphs, stanzas or plots — may pop into your mind. If so, great. Write them down.

Many of these may appear to come out of nowhere. Some will make immediate sense, but others may at first seem inappropriate or irrelevant. *Write them all down regardless.* Often your unconscious will make an intuitive leap that doesn't consciously seem to fit; but as you write the piece that evolves from your associations, the wisdom of this seemingly illogical connection — or, at least, a way to make the connection fit — will eventually reveal itself to you.

When you're finished writing, add your responses to these first two assignments to your notebook. Either copy them over or, if you prefer, simply tape the loose pages directly inside the book.

3. Your responses to the second assignment will be especially useful. Each set of responses will serve as working notes for a complete piece of writing, and will provide a partial description of that piece. Each set will also serve as a springboard to get started, and will give you guidance and direction for completing the piece.

Your final assignment is to look over these responses carefully, then pick a single set of responses to work with. *This will form the basis for your first full-fledged piece of writing.* You'll write this piece from start to finish in Steps 9-21.

In this step you've learned to work with your memories and experiences — and to build on them. You've taught yourself to note significant relationships in your existing material, as well as to forge new ones. You can repeat this process any time you please to discover connections, make associations, come to conclusions, and create the foundation for a new piece of writing.

Forget the "Have-To's"

T hroughout our lives, each of us has been taught a variety of "shoulds," "musts" and "have-to's." While some of these make a great deal of sense ("stop on the red, go on the green"), others are questionable ("eat a hearty breakfast every morning"), and still others are downright nonsense ("always finish one project before starting another").

Some of the "shoulds" that we've learned over the years involve writing. We've learned them from English teachers, from books about writing, from editors, from other writers, and from a variety of other sources.

When it comes to the conventions of grammar, spelling, punctuation and sentence structure, many of these "shoulds" and "musts" make sense. So do the standards for preparing and submitting manuscripts to editors (which I'll discuss in detail in Steps 26 and 28). These conventions and standards, while arbitrary, serve to make reading and writing easier for everyone.

But a great many of the "shoulds," "musts" and "have-to's" that relate to writing are actually quite useless. Often they reflect nothing more than the biases, preferences or ignorance of the people who advocate them. Sometimes they've been simply passed on, unquestioned, from generation to generation. In other cases, they may be useful for some people, but useless or even counterproductive for others.

The best way to deal with these "shoulds" is to get them out into the open, acknowledge them as useless or harmful, and then simply forget them.

What follows is a list of the most common "shoulds," "musts" and "have-to's" that many of us have been taught about writing. Each is either useless, irrelevant or just plain incorrect:

- You should work on only one piece of writing at a time.
- You must write every day, or for a minimum amount of time every day.
- You must write a certain number of words or pages each day.
- If you're serious about writing, you must make it your top priority at all times.
- You must always stick to a strict writing schedule.
- You should have a separate room for writing.
- A writer must be unhappy (or lonely, cynical, 100 percent serious, neurotic, a little crazy or downright nuts).
- If you wish to be published, you must do whatever editors ask.
- You must be completely free from all distractions and interruptions to write well.
- You should stubbornly resist any editor's attempts to change your work.
- You must bare your soul in your writing and/or write about the most personal and intimate details of your life.
- You must dress and act in a certain way, and/or associate with certain people, to be a successful writer.
- You have to know (and/or kowtow to) the right people to be published.
- You should always write an outline before you begin your first draft.
- You must write your title first.
- You must write the various sections of your piece in the same sequence in which they will be read.
- You must know how your piece will end before you begin writing it.
- You must always write "he or she," "him or her" or "his or her" when referring to hypothetical people.
- You should always put the most exciting or important part of your piece at the very beginning, so it will grab your readers.
- You must always begin each piece with something shocking or exciting, or else risk losing your reader.
- Always write a minimum of two (or three, or four, or five) drafts. First drafts will never be any good.
- You must keep each of your manuscripts circulating among editors until it is accepted for publication.
- If a manuscript is rejected, you should get it back out to another editor within twenty-four hours.

- To protect yourself against literary theft, you must register everything you write with the government copyright office, and/or you must mail yourself a copy of each piece as soon as it's completed.
- You must put your social security number, a proper copyright notice (e.g., Copyright 1993 by Scott Edelstein), and the rights you wish to sell on the first page of each of your manuscripts.

The only sane response to any of these pronouncements is a loud and emphatic, *"No!"* None of them is universally true. Some may be useful or true for some writers, or under certain circumstances. Many—the last seven, for example—are sheer baloney.

In addition to the "shoulds," writers also face a barrage of equally worthless "shouldn'ts." Here are the most common examples:

- Never write about yourself.
- Never write in the first person, or use the words *I, me* or *my*.
- Never use curse words, slang or colloquialisms.
- Never use italics.
- Never use exclamation points.
- Never use foreign words.
- Never start a sentence with *and, but, anyway, however, nevertheless, therefore* or *I*.
- Never use incomplete sentences.
- Never stray from correct grammar and usage.
- Never write in dialect; always use standard English.
- Never send a piece you've written to more than one editor at a time.
- Never submit photocopied manuscripts to editors.
- Never rewrite, except to editorial order.

There is yet another type of nonsense that we writers often face: strange beliefs about what makes a writer. It's common for people—usually literature professors, editors, or other writers with overblown egos—to try to tell us who is and isn't a writer. These folks like to proclaim that no one can legitimately call themselves a writer (or, at least, a *real* writer) unless they have done one of the following:

- Written (or published) at least two (or three, or ten, or twenty) books.
- Had at least two (or five, or fifty) pieces published.
- Been writing for at least two (or five, or fifteen) years.

- Written at least a million words.
- Been writing full time, or a certain number of hours per week for a particular number of weeks.
- Worked a variety of jobs, traveled, and/or had plenty of experience with the "real world."
- Read and studied the great works of Western literature.
- Received a Master of Fine Arts degree in writing.
- Suffered.

All of these pronouncements are nothing less than absurd.

If someone says that you must have published at least five books to be a writer, the odds are good that this person has himself published at least five books. And if someone believes that you need to have completed an M.F.A. to be a real writer, I'll bet you dollars to gumballs that she has an M.F.A. diploma hanging on her wall.

I've never quite understood why certain people need to define for the rest of the world who is and isn't a writer. After all, do you know anyone who spends their time explaining to the world which people deserve to be called real plumbers? ("Unless you've fixed at least 250 leaky toilets. . . . ")

It ought to be obvious — at least, it's obvious to me — that anyone who writes is a writer, just as anyone who rides a bicycle is a bicyclist, and anyone who golfs is a golfer. Whether you're an experienced writer, or a professional writer (i.e., someone who makes all or part of their living through writing), or even a talented writer are different questions, of course.

YOUR ASSIGNMENT

This one's easy.

First, photocopy the three lists that appear in this chapter. Then post these lists in a fairly prominent place; hang them on a wall or bulletin board in your work space, or tape them inside your notebook. At the top of each page, write in large letters, "Bad Advice — Ignore." Or, if you prefer, draw a circle with a diagonal line through it on each page.

Second, know these items for what they are: false rumors. Because you may have learned some of them as absolutes when you were younger, you may need to unlearn them. That's why you've posted the lists in a prominent spot: so that you'll see them regularly and remind yourself that you don't have to follow them or believe in them.

Third, ignore these statements when you hear other people declare them, when you read them in books, or when they pop up in your own mind as you write. And some of them *will* pop up now and then, out of sheer habit. When they arise, threatening to get in your way, simply stop for a moment. Check to be sure that what you're thinking is on one of the three lists. Once you've found it, reassure yourself that it's as silly and useless as you thought, and mentally toss that pompous prescription over your shoulder. Then get back to the business of writing.

By now you've bought all the supplies you need. You've set up your work space, started your writer's notebook, discovered several inexhaustible sources of material for your writing, and learned how to access each of those sources at will. You've trained yourself to observe more fully, to focus on what matters to you, and to put together ideas and images in a meaningful way. You've learned to ignore rules that get in your way rather than support and nurture your writing. And, in the process, you've completed Part One of this book.

With these skills and experiences under your belt, you're ready to start writing a story, poem, essay, or other piece of creative writing from start to finish.

PART TWO

Getting the Words Out

Pick a Starting Point

Two of the most common — and most anxiety-producing — questions that beginning writers ask themselves are, "Where do I begin?" and "How do I get started?"

The answer to the first question is quite simple: You can begin anywhere you like. There are no rules, requirements or absolutes.

Writing isn't like playing a piece of music. If you perform a piano concerto, you must play all of the notes and chords in the proper sequence. But if you write an essay, poem or story, nobody will see what you've written until you're ready to show it to them — which means that *you don't have to write your piece in the order in which it is to be read.* You can always arrange and rearrange the parts later.

If you write a short story, for example, you might write the closing paragraph first, then the rest of the final scene, then the first two scenes, and then, as your intuition and desires direct you, the scenes in between.

In some cases, you might not even know how to order your scenes until you've written most or all of them. Many writers, in fact, begin by writing the scenes that most intrigue or excite them, without regard for where they will appear in the finished piece. Only later do they concern themselves with fitting the scenes together.

Other writers like to write the easiest parts of a piece first, then work on the more difficult sections. This enables them to build up momentum quickly, so they can keep writing when the going gets tough.

Your freedom to begin anywhere also refers to the sequence of events, images or ideas that appear in your piece. Suppose, for example, that you decide to write a personal essay chronicling your eight years as a Newfoundland fisherman. You could begin by recounting the day you first stepped onto a fishing boat as a teenager. Or you could begin earlier, with the fascination you felt for the sea as a child—or earlier still, at age four, when you first wondered where the fish on your dinner plate came from.

Or you could begin your essay in the present and use your current perspective to look back on your years as a fisherman. Or you might begin with your last day as a fisherman, comparing it to other working days two, five and eight years earlier.

Beginning your piece anywhere you choose also applies to the specific material that you elect to work with first. You might, for example, decide to start by working with a *character*—your grandfather, say. You could begin by recounting your earliest recollection of him, or by recreating a discussion the two of you had a few weeks ago, or by using your grandfather's voice and viewpoint to describe life in Nazi-occupied France during World War II.

You could also begin writing your piece with a specific *incident, scene* or *event*—either real or imaginary—such as the rescue of two half-drowned children from a flooded basement, the final inning of the 1960 World Series, the landing of the first manned spacecraft on Mars, or the reunion of elderly twin brothers after forty years apart.

Another good place to begin is with a strong *image*, which is a set of sensory impressions. (An image can involve any of the five senses, and often two or three combined.) Some examples: a pair of deer dashing across a highway; the hail rattling against a rusting bulldozer; hot air balloons rising above fields of ripening corn; a Tibetan family sitting, still and silent, in meditation. (William Faulkner's novel *The Sound and the Fury* grew out of a single image that Faulkner had of a small child climbing a tree in her underwear.)

Many successful pieces begin with a *setting*, which is an image that creates a strong sense of place. Examples of settings include: a marsh with morning steam rising from it; the afternoon rush-hour traffic jam on the George Washington bridge; an abandoned cabin overgrown with vines; the glitzy lounge of a cruise ship, heavy with chandeliers and chrome.

It's also possible to begin building your piece around a *theme* or *concept*. Examples here might include: stopping the growth of inner-city gangs; why America should have a democratically elected king and queen; how activists on both sides of the abortion debate believe they are protecting our civilization from barbarism; or why El Paso is a far more American city than Washington, D.C.

Many writers have used a single strong *line*, *statement* or *quotation* as their entrance into a piece. Some examples: "We always had to look good in airports"; "The new moon hangs in the old moon's shadow"; "I smell the coming rain"; "Sometimes I think the whole world is on back order"; "What Velveeta is to cheese, Elizabeth was to nursing." Often — but not necessarily — these become the first or last lines of successful pieces.

You can also begin by outlining a specific *plot*, or sequence of events. Despite what you may have been taught in school, however, you don't *have* to prepare an outline to get started. It's entirely optional — and, for many writers, even counterproductive. (I'll discuss outlines, and some useful variations and alternatives, in Step 10.)

In fact, you don't have to know how or where your finished piece will begin in order to start writing. For that matter, you don't have to know where it will go, how it will end, or even what it will ultimately focus on. Indeed, in many cases it is only *after* you have started writing a piece that you discover where it will go, what it will do, or what it has to say. Writing often comes first, with content, structure and focus coming second.

Mysterious? Yes. Unusual? No, not at all.

This step began with two questions: "Where do I begin?" and "How do I get started?" The answer to the second question is even simpler than the answer to the first: You begin writing by sitting down and putting words on paper. This involves no magic, no special tricks and no complicated training. You just do it, one word, one phrase, one line at a time.

YOUR ASSIGNMENT

Look over all your notes for the first piece you want to write. Based on these notes, pick a basic form or genre (pronounced "zhawń-ruh") to work with: fiction, nonfiction, poetry or prose poetry (poetry written in paragraphs rather than stanzas; see page 114 for a more detailed definition).

Next, pick a specific place to begin writing. This might be a scene or event, an image, a character, a certain viewpoint, a setting, a concept, a quotation, a theme, a line or statement, or anything else that deeply affects you and feels as if it can open up into much more.

Then find a series of blank pages in your notebook and write out this item completely. If it's only one line or sentence, that's fine; if it's an entire scene or stanza, that's even better.

When you've finished writing this beginning, *keep on writing*. Continue until you reach a natural stopping place. Then take a break and turn to Step 10.

Try Outlining, Netlining and Plotting

O ne way to get an excellent start on your piece is to outline it. For many writers, preparing an outline before they begin writing can provide a focus, a direction to follow, and a blueprint to work from.

But outlines aren't for everybody. In fact, for some writers they're confining and stultifying. They'd much rather just begin writing, letting themselves discover what they have to say as they write. Outlining, then, is an option — not a requirement — for anyone who wants to write. This step is entirely optional as well.

By the way, I am not talking here about the kind of formal outline you probably wrote in high school, in which you organized an essay according to topics, subtopics, sub-subtopics and so on, until you wanted to run screaming from the classroom. For your purposes, an outline can be any set of notes that sketches out the potential structure, plot, direction, or movement of your piece.

Here are some legitimate and useful ways to outline a piece of creative writing:

- A simple list (perhaps numbered 1, 2, 3, 4, 5, etc.) of topics that you're thinking of covering, key points you plan to make, or scenes, sections or stanzas you plan to write. If you like, you may add notes or a description to each item on your list.
- A narrative synopsis of your plot — in essence, a highly condensed version of your piece, written in prose.
- A narrative description of what your piece will do or be.
- A flow chart showing the movement of events, characters, ideas, points, topics, images and/or relationships, from the beginning of your piece to the end.
- A *netline* — also called a *mind map* — is an ingenious form of

outlining that focuses on relationships rather than sequence, and that presents information visually rather than in a linear fashion. A netline often resembles a spider web or a net (hence its name).

To begin a netline of your own, start with a blank piece of unlined paper (or a blank page in your writer's notebook) and the set of responses from Step 7 that you've chosen to work with. In the middle of the blank page, write down the central premise, point, image, intention, character, metaphor or event of your piece. If your piece has more than a single primary focus, note each one near the center of the page, leaving at least an inch between items. If you're not sure yet what will form the core of your piece, leave the middle of the page blank; about two inches from the center (in any direction), note the most important elements you've come up with so far, again leaving an inch or so between items.

Then, farther out from the center, write down other, less significant elements for your piece. If one of these relates closely to something already on the page, place it nearby; if it's entirely new or unrelated, locate it farther away.

Continue this process until you feel your netline is complete. If ideas and images occur to you as your netline develops, feel free to add them.

As your netline takes shape, relationships among many of its elements will emerge. Indicate these relationships by drawing lines or arrows between the appropriate items. If lines cross or converge, that's fine. Some items will quickly become hubs, with many lines or arrows radiating out of (or leading to) them.

As more and more connections emerge, you may need to relocate some items, and perhaps even redraw your netline entirely. You may also want to use a larger page—for instance, a page from an artist's sketchbook.

When your netline is finished, it will show you at a glance how all the major elements of your piece relate to one another. It may also reveal connections and relationships that you hadn't realized were there.

I've included two sample netlines on pages 44 and 45. The first is for a short essay on prison overcrowding; the second is for a poem about a romance between a master chef and her assistant. As netlines go, they're both rather logical and orderly, so don't be surprised if the netlines you develop look looser and more jumbled.

- Any other set of notes that helps you organize your ideas or plan your piece.

If you feel that a formal outline (with its categories and subcategories, and its use of the symbols I, II, III, A, B, C, etc.) can be genuinely useful, by all means feel free to prepare one.

Whatever type of outline you use, think of it as tentative. If, as you write, a new direction or emphasis occurs to you, feel free to try it out. If it works, continue to follow it; if it doesn't, simply return to your original plan. Feel free to amend your outline as your piece—and your thinking about it—grows and changes.

Although outlines and netlines primarily assist writers in producing first drafts, they can also be useful in other ways. For example, you might write a draft or two first, then prepare an outline or netline of what you've written already. This can help you sort out your thoughts and see patterns and relationships that you might otherwise have missed. It can also give you a better grasp of where your piece is succeeding and where it still needs work.

One writer I know finds it useful to prepare an outline or netline when she's stuck in the middle of a draft. This enables her to see more clearly where the problems in her piece lie and what she can do to get it moving again.

As you might guess, different writers like different outlining techniques. Sometimes a certain approach works best for one piece, and a different one works best for another. Some writers have even found it useful to outline the same piece in more than one way. Still other writers (I, for one) will sometimes outline first, sometimes netline first, and sometimes start writing without any preparation at all, depending on what we're writing and what our guts tell us.

All of the outlining techniques described in this step work equally well for stories, poems, essays, and other forms of creative writing.

YOUR ASSIGNMENT

This is the one step that's optional. It's a suggestion, not a requirement.

If you've not yet begun to write your piece, outline or netline it first, using one or more of the techniques described in this step. If you're not sure which approach to try, pick the one that feels the most comfortable, promising or intriguing; if for some reason it doesn't bear fruit, try another. Keep your outline near as you write your first draft.

If you've already written part or all of a first draft, outline or netline what you've finished so far. Then look over your outline carefully. What does it tell you about your piece — and the elements that make it up — that you didn't know before? Do you see any new relationships, associations or connections?

If your attempts to outline or netline your piece get you nowhere — or if the very idea of outlining makes you stiffen up — simply skip this step. Write your piece by letting it reveal itself to you one line or sentence at a time.

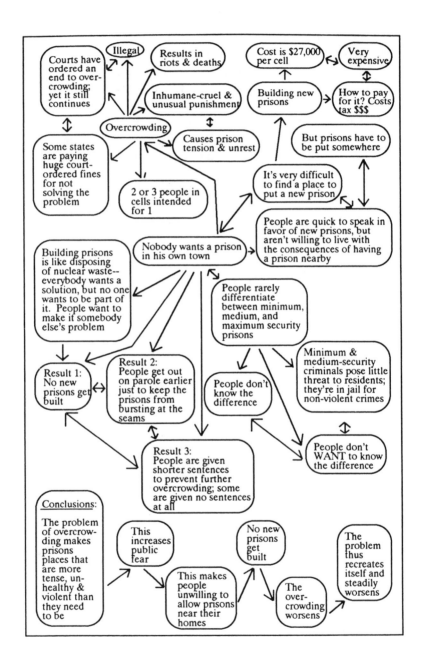

Narrator is Susan, a middle-aged master chef and restaurant owner.

She hires Mario as her kitchen assistant. He's 29, just out of chef's school. His first career was as an accountant.

Poem focuses on their affair.

1. She interviews him for job, tells him her restaurant's her whole life, asks why he gave up accounting. He says, "I wanted to sink my hands into something. I wanted to honor my body and my tongue." She hires him.

2. Mario's smart and talented and quick. Too quick--his second day on the job, in a hurry, he knocks a handful of change into a mixer. He thinks he got all the coins out, but next morning, eating a muffin, Susan bites into a quarter.

3. Five nights later, a huge group of wealthy people arrives just before closing. They spend lots of money, love the food, stay hours past closing time, leave a $50 bill as a special tip for the chefs. Susan asks Mario, "How should we split this?" He suggests a bottle of Dom Perignon from the cellar, at cost. They drink it and get tipsy. He spills champagne on her neck, says, "If you close early you can lose your best customers," leans forward, kisses her. They fall onto the counter, sending menus flying.

4. Their affair continues in the restaurant. They leave notes for each other on blank restaurant checks about when and where to meet to make love: Party room, 2 p.m., Office, 9 p.m., the meat locker, the roof. On the roof, they picnic on paper-wrapped chicken, then let their clothing drop away. Afterward, she asks him to take her home with him. He balks. She forces the issue; finally he says, "I can't."

FOOD   MONEY   SLIPS/SHEETS OF PAPER   SPILLING/DROPPING   MOUTH/TONGUE

5. They close up the restaurant for the night; he kisses her and leaves. Feeling ashamed, she follows him home, already knowing what she'll find. From a distance, she sees his wife and kids come outside to greet him, carrying what looks like a birthday cake. She drives away.

6. Next day, doing accounts, she realizes the restaurant's losing money. Mario appears behind her, places his hand on her shoulder. "I doubt you're breaking even," he says. "Too many cooks." She removes his hand, asks, "Where's your wedding ring?" He steps back, shrugs. "I took it off to make sausage a year ago. Never saw it again." "Why did you seduce me?" "I wanted you."

7. Three days later he quits; he's taken a job as a sous chef across town. He tries to kiss her good-bye; she refuses, hands him his final paycheck. "You should have a professional look over those accounts," he says, and goes.

8. After interviewing people for Mario's job, she hires a talented middle-aged woman. She calls her second choice, a young man in his thirties, tells him apologetically that she's given the job to someone else. He thanks her, hesitates, asks her to dinner. He pauses again, asks, "Or are you busy cooking every night?" "Of course not," she says. "Do you think this restaurant is my whole life?"

Write a First Draft

E ach version of a piece of writing is called a *draft*. A *first draft* is your initial attempt at writing your piece more or less from beginning to end.

Your first draft will probably bear only a passing resemblance to the final draft you'll eventually write. Much of your first draft will be awkward, sketchy and unfocused—but that's normal. A first draft isn't supposed to be polished or flawless—it's just supposed to give you something solid and substantial to work with.

Here are the two most important items to keep in mind when writing a first draft:

1. Your guiding principles at all times should be the questions "What moves, intrigues or fascinates me?" and "What do I want to say, do, see or have happen in this piece?"

2. Your primary focus should be on getting the words on the page (or on the computer screen). Keep the flow going.

Don't worry about getting things exactly right in your initial draft. That will come later, with subsequent drafts, revision and/or editing. If you can't come up with quite the right word, phrase, image or connection, spend a brief amount of time—a minute at most— searching for it. But if the right words don't come, don't get bogged down looking for them. Make a note to yourself in the appropriate spot (e.g., "stronger image of decay here," "make dialogue angrier," etc.), or simply leave a blank space. Then move on to the next sentence or line. After your first draft is complete, you can come back, focus your full attention on the difficult passage, and work with it until it sounds and feels just right.

It can be tempting to edit, censor or critique your words as they flow out. *Resist this temptation and keep writing.* Don't distract yourself from your task of creating a complete (if imperfect) version of your piece. Once you have a *considerable* amount of writing experience, you can experiment with alternate writing processes.

At times what you write may strike you as vague, or awkward, or confusing, or shocking, or silly, or just plain wrong. That's okay; let it be that way. Remind yourself that you'll have plenty of opportunity to work on it later. Just keep writing.

As your piece develops, words, phrases, images and ideas may come to you completely out of the blue. Some of these may work in strange or surprising ways. If they sound or feel right, by all means use them. If you're not sure about them, however, jot them down and continue in the direction you've been going. You may find a use for them later — or they may provide a solution if you find yourself getting lost or stuck.

It's possible that, despite your plans and intentions, your piece may start to take off in a new and unexpected direction, seemingly of its own accord. This is both common and natural: Pieces of writing often change and evolve as they're being created. Keep in mind that you're not obliged to stick to your original plan or structure; if a new focus, theme, viewpoint or direction emerges, feel free to explore it. Trust your hunches and intuition here: If something feels right, it's probably worth trying. If it doesn't take you anywhere worthwhile, or the piece starts to change into something you don't want it to become, you can always return to your original plan.

There may also be times when you simply don't know what to do or where to go next. You may find yourself at a crossroads, with two or more options to choose from, and with no clear choice making itself apparent. Or you might feel lost or stuck, with no idea at all what your next step should be. In either of these cases, simply ask yourself once again, "What do I most want to see, do, say or have happen here? What will most move, excite or interest me?" Your answer should provide you with a clear direction.

If it doesn't, however, stop writing for the moment. Often it helps to take your cues from what you've already written — so go back and reread your notes for the piece you're working on. Then read over what you've written in the first draft so far. Follow whatever ideas, hunches or gut reactions come to you.

If contemplation doesn't get you going again, open up your writer's notebook and scan its pages. Chances are excellent that something you've recorded in it will provide the right creative spark.

If, despite all your efforts, you still find yourself stuck, don't despair. There are a variety of strategies for getting yourself unstuck. Try one or more of the following:

- Rewrite or retype your last page, then keep going.
- Write something else for a while—preferably something that comes easily to you, such as a letter or a notebook entry.
- Change how, when or where you write. Sometimes a change in your scenery, schedule or work habits can give you a new perspective.
- Stop writing, but don't leave your work space. Sit quietly for several minutes, deliberately *not* thinking about your piece and *not* trying to solve your problem. Follow your breath in and out of your body, and let your mind wander. For the next half hour, observe what bubbles up naturally into your consciousness; if something seems promising, write it down.
- Give yourself a time-out, and take your mind off the subject for a while. Take a walk, see a movie, eat lunch or take a nap. Then return to your piece refreshed.
- Promise yourself some kind of a reward once you've solved your problem—and be sure to give yourself this reward after you've found a solution or direction.
- Brainstorm with one or more other people for new ideas, directions and approaches.
- If you work well under pressure, set a reasonable deadline for getting unstuck—say, forty-five or sixty minutes. Then stick to it.
- If necessary, put the piece aside for a day or two. Give your conscious mind a rest and your unconscious a chance to work on the problem.

Unless you plan to write a very short piece, don't expect to write a full first draft in a single sitting. You may need several writing sessions to produce a complete draft.

In each writing session, work until you feel your time, energy, inspiration or enthusiasm beginning to run low. Then go a little longer, until you come to a natural stopping place. When you reach this point, quit writing. Spend the next five to ten minutes making notes on where the piece will go next, what it will do, and what it will include. Finish your writing session by rereading everything you've done on your piece so far.

What do you do if, after working on your piece for some time, you realize that you've lost all interest in it? Simple: Put that piece aside (but *don't* throw it away!) and choose a new piece to work on. Then write a full first draft of this new poem, story or essay.

YOUR ASSIGNMENT

Write a complete first draft of the piece you've chosen to work on. Follow the tips and guidance in this step.

Steps 12-16 will also help you write this initial version of your piece. Please read them now—or, if you prefer, alternate between reading these steps and writing portions of your piece.

Engage Your Reader's Senses

O ur senses are the instruments through which we perceive the world. Indeed, it is only through our powers of sight, hearing, touch, smell and taste that we can connect with external reality. Our perceptions provide us with information that enables us to construct a multisensory picture of the world inside our heads.

This has profound significance for us. As creative writers, whose only tools are words, we must create (or recreate) the world inside our readers' heads. To create this mental world, we must give our readers sensory information; we must describe everything in terms of what we can smell, hear, touch, see and taste.

Each set of related sensory details is called an *image*. Most of us tend to think of images as visual—for instance, red and yellow streamers blowing in a breeze, morning fog rising from a lake, or a dog baring its teeth. But images can involve any of the senses. The tremolo of a loon; the smell of burning leaves; the smooth, cool texture of marble; and the sharp, sweet taste of licorice—all these are images.

An image can also combine two or more different senses. Some examples: ten elderly women laughing and splashing each other in a heavily chlorinated swimming pool; a wet, mewing kitten trying to climb your bare leg, its tiny claws digging into your skin; a perky, smartly dressed department store manager giving a pep talk to three dozen novice Santa Clauses. Combining information from two or more senses often creates the most vivid images and results in the most intense and affecting experiences for readers.

Most of us have been taught to respond primarily to visual images. Actually, though, human beings' most acute and powerful sense is our sense of smell. Our strongest memories are frequently of odors and aromas, and often a single smell can evoke several vivid and highly detailed recollections. For example, the smell of cotton candy always evokes for me strong, clear images of an amusement park on a hot summer day.

To some degree, all of our senses except sight have been underused. As you write, keep in mind that all five senses connect us to the world.

It's not enough to simply provide sensory information, however; you must provide the specific information that captures the essence of what you describe. *Knowing how to pick just the right sensory details is at the heart of good writing.* This is easier to do than it sounds — in fact, most of us do it every day in our speaking and thinking.

For example, let's consider the object I'm looking at right now. If I told you it was ugly and boring but functional (and it is all three), you'd have no idea what it is. But if I said that it squats in the corner of my office, gurgling, hissing and giving off heat, chances are that you could identify it as a radiator. You are able to do this because I gave you specific information about how it looks (it "squats in the corner of my office"), what it sounds like ("gurgling, hissing"), and what it feels like ("giving off heat") — and you used that information to create a multisensory picture in your mind.

This worked because I gave you in words the same sensory information you would receive by observing the radiator yourself. More important, I selected the *right* pieces of sensory information, the ones that enabled you to form a complete mental picture. I could just as accurately have described the radiator as a solid, heavy object with gray peeling paint and a knob on one end, or as a four-legged set of pipes held together with a threaded metal rod — but none of this information would have captured the essence of what a radiator is.

Let's return to my first description of the radiator. In this description I used the words *ugly, boring* and *functional,* none of which is very helpful. In fact, these words don't really describe the radiator in my office at all; instead they describe *my judgments about* the radiator.

No object or person is inherently ugly, boring or functional. After all, a painting that one person finds ugly another may think is beautiful. I enjoy Woody Allen's films; my wife finds most of them boring. And while I might say that my cat is functional because she kills mice that get into my home, does she stop being functional when all of the mice have been killed?

There's nothing wrong with making such judgments, of course, or with including them in your writing. But don't confuse judgments with sensory details. Look at these two lists of words:

tingling	fantastic
ochre	harmonious
mossy	attractive
stiff	unappealing
cracked	unique
sweating	nasty
bitter	ordinary
screeching	delicious
musky	miserable

Each word in the left-hand column provides specific sensory information, through which your reader can create a clear internal picture. In contrast, the words on the right represent someone's evaluations, opinions or judgments. They are one step removed from sensory experience.

If I tell you I ate a delicious lunch this afternoon, you have no idea what I ate. It could be pizza, chowder or Caesar salad. I haven't shown you *anything* about my meal—I've only told you my opinion of it. But if I say, "I had deep-fried bean curd with sauteed broccoli and roasted cashews in garlic sauce," not only do you know exactly what I ate, but you'll have some idea of what it looked, smelled and tasted like, because I've given you enough sensory details for you to create a picture in your mind. I've also allowed you to have your own opinion of bean curd, which you may or may not think of as delicious.

I don't mean to give you the impression, however, that the more sensory details you present, the better. It's not a question of amount, but of appropriateness. To paraphrase one of Douglas Adams's characters, you need to put in the right bits and throw the other bits away.

Consider this sentence: "Taking the long, sharp, gleaming metal hoe, she planted her bare feet firmly on the dusty path, inhaled noisily—the phlegm in her sinuses making her wheeze a bit—and struck the green, slithering snake just behind its slightly uplifted head." This sentence is so overloaded with sensory information that you don't know which details to focus on, or which are meant to be significant. The trick is to present the most significant details—the ones that reveal the *essence* of the person, object, action or situation.

When you present your reader with sensory information, you *show* them people, objects, settings and events, rather than merely tell about them. Consider the following two passages: (1) *Shannon was excited.* (2) *Shannon pushed her way to the front of the cheering crowd. She knocked a string of balloons off a table, climbed on top and shouted, "It's a goddamn miracle!"* The first sentence *tells* the reader how Shannon feels but fails to bring the reader into the scene; the second *shows* the reader exactly what's happening and allows them to see, feel and even share in Shannon's excitement.

Notice, by the way, that in the second passage the word *excited* doesn't appear anywhere. There's no need for it, because the passage shows what Shannon is doing; her emotions come through loud and clear.

In creative writing, showing is almost always preferable to telling, unless you are trying to make a quick transition from one scene, time, location, viewpoint or topic to another.

Incidentally, everything I've written in this chapter applies as much to nonfiction as it does to poetry or fiction. To see how these principles work in nonfiction, let's look at a few sentences from one of Annie Dillard's nonfiction books, *The Writing Life*, in which she observes the flight of a sphinx moth:

> After trembling so violently that it seemed it must blow apart, the moth took flight. Its wings blurred, like a hummingbird's. It flew a few yards out over the water before it began losing altitude. It was going down. Its wings buzzed; it gained height and lost, gained and lost, and always lost more than it gained, until its heavy body dragged in the water, and it drowned before my eyes with a splash.

No matter what genre you work in, the more you focus on providing the right sensory details—and the more that you are specific, clear and concrete—the more likely you are to engage and affect your readers.

YOUR ASSIGNMENT

As you write, imagine that what you're writing about is actually happening, right before you, right now. Play it out inside your head, as if it were a movie. Follow it from beginning to end, moment by moment, and write down what you observe—what you hear, what you see, and, if appropriate, what you smell, taste or touch. Focus on sensory details, and try to home in on just the right ones.

Don't expect to be able to do this well in every line or sentence, however. Finding the right details or images isn't always easy, especially in a first draft. If an image that feels right doesn't come, *don't stop writing.* Leave a blank space, or make some notes, or temporarily use an image that's not quite right; then move on. Only later, once your draft is complete, should you come back and work on that image further.

Remember to show things to your reader rather than merely tell about them — particularly in the case of emotions. Instead of writing, "I was furious," *show* yourself being furious. For example: *"Forget it!" I shouted, grabbing my books. I stormed out of the bedroom, slammed the door behind me, and ran down the steps before I could have second thoughts.*

Your ability to find and use the right sensory details will get steadily better with time and practice. And remember: You already use this kind of detail every day in your speaking and thinking.

Let Yourself Fantasize

A s you learned in Step 11, all you really need to do when writing a first draft is get some words, images and ideas onto the page (or the computer screen) in front of you. This gives you an enormous amount of freedom — freedom to invent, to play and to fantasize.

Most of us spend quite a bit of our time fantasizing. In fact, by the time we reach adulthood, we've become experts at it. Virtually anything that's pleasurable or painful can get our imaginations going. So can the *lack* of stimulus: When we're bored, we daydream.

This ability to imagine and fantasize can help sharpen and strengthen your writing; it can add impact, insight and intensity. And because this ability comes so naturally, you can put it to work in your writing quickly and easily. Often all you need to do is let your mind loose and follow it wherever it goes — or, at most, ask yourself a simple but provocative question, such as, "What's most frightening about the house?" or "What if the car were to have a flat tire halfway home?"

Suppose, for example, that in your first draft of a short story, you've written a scene in which your narrator visits her seriously ill grandmother in the hospital. You could simply describe the sterile hospital room and leave it at that. But what if, instead of merely describing what you see, you let go of your mental reins and let your imagination lead you? Here are two examples of what you might come up with:

1. She seemed tiny and shrunken in the big, tightly made hospital bed. Her face was damp with sweat, but someone had tucked the blanket under her chin, as if to hold her in place. The bed looked like a huge mouth waiting patiently to swallow her.

2. The room was small, dark and uncomfortably quiet. Ellen lay asleep in the bed, breathing shallowly, as if even while unconscious she was afraid to disturb the dark, heavy silence. I pictured the room slowly shrinking with each passing hour, her breath growing steadily shallower, until at last the darkness and silence were complete, and the room had become a coffin.

In each of these cases, I first created a basic setting, then allowed my mind to play with it, alter it and fantasize about it. The result in each case was an unusual and — I hope — disturbing image.

Fantasizing doesn't only lend itself to the writing of fiction and poetry. It can be just as powerful a tool if you're creating nonfiction — even serious, analytical, down-to-earth nonfiction. Consider the following example, noting in particular the final image:

Despite his insistence that balancing the state's budget would be a top priority during his first term as governor, in his first year in office he supported a $52 million increase in state spending. His compatriots argued that this increase was actually quite modest, since the state's total budget has exceeded $15 billion each year for more than a decade. But consider this: if fifty-two million one dollar bills were placed atop the state capitol building, the capitol dome would immediately crumble under their weight.

Fantasizing often works by adding a twist — a new perspective, approach, connection, emphasis or association.

One of the best ways to fantasize as you write is to ask yourself the question *What if?* The potential variations on this question are limitless. Some examples: "What if she had arrived ten minutes earlier?" "What if he hit her instead of kissed her?" "What if this had happened during medieval times?" "What if the doorbell were to suddenly ring — and who would it be?" "What if she saw a galloping horse instead of a trotting dog?" "What if his 'skiing accident' were actually a self-inflicted injury?" "What if it were night?" "What if Nathan were poor instead of well-to-do?" "What if this were narrated by Gwendolyn instead of written in the third person?" "What if this had taken place in a matriarchal culture?"

You've been developing your ability to daydream and fantasize all your life. With a little practice, you'll soon be able to use this skill to make your writing stronger and deeper.

YOUR ASSIGNMENT

As you create your first draft, let your imagination loose. Instead of writing what's most likely to happen or the image your reader is most expecting, give yourself free rein to visualize, to imagine and to dream.

If your ability to fantasize doesn't kick in automatically, simply ask yourself one or more of these questions:

- What's the best thing that could happen in my piece right now? The most exciting? The most appropriate?
- What's the worst thing that could possibly happen now? The most painful? The most unlucky? The most dangerous? The most frightening?
- What's the single most unexpected thing that might happen now? The strangest? The most incongruous?
- What's the funniest thing that could happen right now?
- What does the person, object, image or action I'm writing about remind me of? How? Why? What does it sound like? Look like? Smell like? Feel like?
- What if _____ ? (Fill in the blank.)

It is of course possible to come up with more than one response to any of these questions.

You're by no means obliged to use whatever fantasy you come up with. If what you visualize doesn't feel right, simply ignore it, and begin fantasizing in another direction — or, if you prefer, ask yourself a different question.

Combine Diverse Elements

O ne of the best ways to intensify, vivify and energize your writing is to bring together two or more things that wouldn't normally be associated with one another. The late Arthur Koestler called this process *bisociation*, and it is one of the simplest and most effective writing techniques.

Here are some examples of bisociation:

- A snowman in a tanning booth.
- A sign in the window of a funeral home that reads, "Today's special: free toaster with every cremation."
- This line in a poem: "Then you left, cutting the roots of your promise."
- This paragraph: "All I ever really wanted in life was to dress in white and be surrounded by bright light. *I should have become a Hindu*, I thought, *or a dentist.*"
- A race of highly intelligent, technologically advanced aliens from another planet, all of whom move their lips when they read.

Even titles can be examples of bisociation. Nicole Niemi wrote a lovely poem called "Wallace Stevens at the Auto Show"; the title of the poem melds the refined (Wallace Stevens, a highly regarded poet) and the crass (the glitz and bluster of an auto show).

Then there is *trisociation*, which is the bringing together of *three* diverse elements into a single event, image, situation or idea. Here's an example of a trisociative premise for a poem or story: A professional bowler has a profound spiritual experience, becomes an itinerant Zen monk, and dedicates her life to driving her R.V. from one bowling alley to another, teaching bowlers how to become one with the pins. (The first line of such a piece might be, "Buddha would have made a great bowler.")

Why are bisociation and trisociation so powerful and effective? Because they enable readers to look at things in new ways, to see connections and relationships that they wouldn't normally see. *Bisociation widens and deepens your readers' vision of the world.*

Not only can bisociation make your writing richer and deeper, but the act of bisociating can help you see things in new and different ways. Bisociation can lead you deeper into your piece — and into your own heart and mind — by transforming and expanding your vision.

Bisociation doesn't have to be as obvious or overt as in the above examples, however. There are other, more subtle ways in which two or more elements can be combined to add strength and vision to your work. Often, in fact, the act of bisociation can be completely invisible to readers.

You might, for example, combine the attributes of two or more places to create a new setting more vivid and moving than any of the originals. Suppose you're writing a poem in which the daughter of a retired steelworker walks through an abandoned steel mill. Perhaps you've wandered through several abandoned factories yourself over the years, and you've accumulated quite a mental library of images from them. Instead of simply choosing one specific factory to use as the setting for your poem, you might pick the ten most striking images and combine them into a single (fictitious) setting. If you like, you can add entirely made-up images as well.

Let's look at another example. You might choose to combine the personality traits of several people you know to create a single character. Suppose you're writing a story about a young policewoman's first day on the job. You might give her the quick, stiff movements of your mother; the anxious grimness of your cousin Terry; your neighbor's compulsive gum-chewing; and the low-key deadpan humor of your best friend's gardener — as well as a variety of other traits of your own invention.

Here's another example, this one combining incidents and events. Suppose you're writing an essay about how little American elementary schools have actually changed over the past forty years. In relating a typical day in a third-grade classroom, you might blend some incidents from your own childhood, an anecdote from a recent newspaper article, and stories told to you by your brother, your boss and several schoolteacher friends.

Two of the examples above—the ones that create a place (the abandoned steel mill) and a character (the rookie policewoman) demonstrate an additional form of bisociation: They combine the real and the imaginary. This melding of memory and imagination can often result in some of the strongest, most moving writing.

While bisociation and trisociation can be used at any time, they can be especially helpful when your piece starts to drag or lose its way. When a first draft begins to bog down, often what it needs is the extra burst of energy or insight that bisociation can provide.

YOUR ASSIGNMENT

As you compose your first draft, look for opportunities to make connections and associations through bisociation and trisociation.

One excellent way to do this is to keep all your responses to the assignments in Step 7 near you as you write. Scan these briefly at opportune moments, such as:

- Before each writing session.
- If you're unsure what to do or where to go next.
- If you find your piece falling into a clichéd or predictable pattern.
- If your writing feels flat or low on energy, or if it seems to be going nowhere.
- If you begin to lose interest in your piece.

When a bisociation or trisociation works, you'll know it immediately, because the line, idea, image, event or other connection will leap out at you. Whenever such an association feels right, use it.

Exaggerate, Embellish and Enlarge

I t's been said that all good writing tells the truth—not always the literal truth, but some emotional or perceptual truth. When Dylan Thomas wrote of "the force that through the green fuse drives the flower," he was describing in poetic terms the inexorable life-force that compels each living thing to survive and grow. He was expressing a truth in words that, if taken literally, would seem absurd and patently untrue.

Of course, it doesn't even occur to us as we read this line of poetry that Thomas was speaking in any way other than metaphorically. We don't expect a completely literal and realistic description because we're reading a poem, not a news article.

We grant this freedom—the freedom to abandon the literal truth in order to express emotional or imagistic truths—not only to poets, but also to fiction writers, playwrights and other creative writers. We allow these people to rewrite reality, to stretch the truth and even to lie, so long as what they write moves us, entertains us, or fulfills us in some way. We care about the human lives, emotions, perceptions and deeds that a successful literary work reveals to us— not about whether it accurately recounts actual events.

What does all of this mean to you as a writer? Just this: As you write your piece, feel free to lie, to exaggerate, to blow things out of proportion, to go to extremes, to pretend, to play, to be outrageous. In fact, in creative writing (as opposed to reporting) virtually anything goes, so long as it has the *feel* of truth to it—i.e., so long as it moves your readers.

Actually, much of the world's best writing is based on exaggeration, embellishment and altered reality. Think of the works of Edgar Allan Poe, or of George Orwell's *1984*, or Miguel de Cervantes' *Don Quixote*. Or think of Herman Melville's *Moby Dick*—a novel so outrageous that when it was first published, two different reviewers insisted that Melville was insane and needed to be locked up.

The best contemporary writing also often relies on stretching or bending the literal truth in order to express important truths of a different kind. Consider Margaret Atwood's *The Handmaid's Tale* (in which women's role in society is reduced to that of servant and breeder), or the poetry of Sylvia Plath, or Gabriel Garcia Marquez's *One Hundred Years of Solitude*, or almost anything by Dave Barry.

As a creative writer, you have enormous freedom—freedom to do whatever moves your readers, no matter how far removed from conventional reality it may be. You possess a license to lie—and, paradoxically, a responsibility to tell the truth.

As your first draft progresses, feel free to make things bigger, or smaller, or faster, or scarier, or more painful, or more pleasurable, or stranger than they ordinarily would be (or than they actually *are*). If you originally envisioned a man with a missing toe, ask yourself if it would be better if he were missing a foot, or even a leg. If you're basing your piece on a real-life incident that began with a knock on the door, maybe the door should instead be flung open, or go up in flames, or explode. If your original plan was to show forty school children splashing in a pond, consider putting something else in the pond with them—perhaps their school bus, stopped at the pond's edge in a foot of water; or several mating dogs from a nearby farm; or thousands of chunks of ice from a sudden summer hailstorm; or half a dozen rusting gumball machines, dumped from the bridge above several months before.

One excellent way to add power and focus to a piece is to give it such an extra twist or turn—to take things one step further, push the tension one notch higher, build momentum one more step, or add one more detail, image or element. In this process you may find yourself naturally fantasizing, bisociating or combining the unreal with the real.

Surprising as it may sound, the above advice applies to a lot of nonfiction as well as to fiction and poetry. It's quite permissible to exaggerate or bend the truth in most articles and essays, provided you indicate clearly (at least via context or implication) that you're doing so. Consider this example from an essay by Lewis H. Lapham that appeared in *Harper's*, noting in particular the final sentence:

The bleak comedy of the autumn presidential campaign followed from the attempts to fit the candidates — both of them nervous government clerks — with the masks of wisdom and power. At their respective nominating conventions in New York and Houston, Governor Clinton and President Bush dutifully invoked the holy names of God and Elvis Presley, but it was clear from the tenor of their remarks that as between the two deities they placed their greater trust in the one with the rhinestones and the electric guitar. It was equally obvious that neither they nor their stage managers would have had much trouble with the question of endorsements. Offered a choice of photo opportunities, they plainly would have preferred to appear with the king at Graceland than with Christ at Golgotha or Gethsemane.

This freedom to exaggerate does not apply, however, to news articles, corporate reports and other pieces where your responsibility as a writer is to present the bare facts as clearly and objectively as possible.

While having a license to lie allows you to try almost anything, it *doesn't* mean that whatever you try will always work. If you push things *too* far, you can actually undermine your piece. You can become absurd or silly when you mean to be dramatic; your characters can start to border on stereotypes or caricatures; you can undercut instead of heighten your impact, emotion or mood; or you can simply lose your reader's trust or interest. (Remember, though, that you're only writing a first draft; if you *do* go too far, you can always scale things back or rewrite that portion of your piece later.)

While it's fine to exaggerate and embellish on people, settings, objects, images and events, you should *not* embellish your writing style. *Good writing is as clear, concise, simple and straightforward as possible.* This principle applies to all forms of writing, including — perhaps especially — poetry. As you write your first draft, avoid verbal tricks, gimmicks and flourishes unless they are genuinely essential to what you are trying to do. Use standard American English except when you have good reason not to; and when you *do* have good reason not to (e.g., when you work with certain metaphors, connections, leaps, quotations, dialects or dialogue), bend the rules only as much as you have to. Don't embellish for the sake of embellishment, or simply to be clever, novel or weird. If you genuinely need to get complex, detailed or circuitous, that's fine—but only get as complex, detailed or circuitous as absolutely necessary.

None of this means, by the way, that you *must* play fast and loose with objective reality as you write. It's possible to write an excellent piece by adhering strictly to everyday events, expectations and language. Indeed, many excellent pieces have been published that do nothing more than relate actual experiences and incidents.

One more point about embellishment: As novelist Donald West-lake has pointed out, "The fictioneer labors under the restraint of plausibility; his inventions must stay within the capacity of the audience to accept and believe. God, of course, working with facts, faces no such limitation." Often our everyday reality can seem so strange, so rife with coincidence and connections, or so perfectly arranged and plotted out that if you were to simply report the events that took place, no one would believe you. You'd be accused of heavy-handedness, of factitiousness, or of manipulating your characters (and, perhaps, your readers). In these cases, you may need to *de-embellish*—that is, to tone down or rewrite what actually happened to make it believable to your readers. This may feel awkward at first, but in fact it is no different from making things larger than life: You present images, ideas and events in an amended way so that they express emotional and perceptual truths.

YOUR ASSIGNMENT

In your first draft, feel free to play with the truth. Deliberately veer away from what your reader might expect. Exaggerate, lie or make up things; alter, twist or transform reality. Skew details, turn them on their sides, or change some of their essential qualities.

If, as you write, you find your piece beginning to lose energy, become predictable or feel sluggish, perhaps a slight (or more than slight) change of direction is what you need. Follow the suggestions throughout this step and see where your efforts take you.

Avoid the Most Common Writing Mistakes

The mistakes I'll discuss in this chapter aren't errors of grammar, punctuation, spelling or sentence structure. All writers make these small errors, and since they're easily fixed with some careful editing and proofreading, they should be of no concern to you as you compose your first draft. It's more important to keep the words coming — so leave the fine tuning for later.

In this step I won't deal with problems such as wordiness, overwriting, unnecessary repetition or awkward pacing, either. These, too, are all quite natural in a first draft, and often in later drafts as well. Because they're problems of degree or balance, they are rarely serious. Fixing them is much like adjusting the valves in an engine or adding flour to some tasty but runny pancake batter.

The mistakes I'll talk about here are basic — and potentially serious — errors of conception or presentation. They are problems that can point your piece in the wrong direction, undermine your basic intent, or confuse or alienate your readers.

In a very real sense, of course, *nothing* in a first draft is ever really a mistake, since you can always revise it later. Indeed, sometimes it's downright necessary to write something badly the first time around in order to write it well the next. I frequently write first drafts in which very little works well, just to get some words, ideas and images on paper. This initial draft provides me with a general structure and a set of working notes to help me write the draft that follows. Even if I end up using little or nothing from my first draft, writing it was nevertheless an essential part of the process of composing a finished, successful piece.

The point isn't to try to get everything right the first time, but to write the best first draft you can, recognize what further work needs to be done, and revise, edit and proofread as much as necessary.

There are, however, a number of common traps that new writers (and many experienced ones as well) frequently fall into. Being alert to these problems in advance can be enormously helpful, because when your piece goes astray, you'll be able to catch yourself and redirect your efforts. Better still, you'll be able to avoid many of the traps in the first place.

As you write, then, keep an eye out for these all-too-common pitfalls:

Trying to do or say too much. It's important to keep your focus narrow and specific in any short piece, particularly an essay. If you try to cover too much ground or jam in too many events or images, you'll confuse your readers and ultimately distance them from your piece. Don't try to sum up the history of Europe in a two-page poem, or discuss all the problems of modern life in a single brief essay, or squeeze three murders, a rape and a robbery into one five-page story.

Dealing in universals or generalities. While it's certainly fine to write about concepts such as love, greed, justice, war or ignorance, writing about them as abstract entities rarely works; it usually results in cold, distant, abstruse pieces that leave readers unmoved. On the other hand, you *can* move and involve your readers by focusing on specific examples—e.g., a particular act of love or greed, a certain battle or court case, or a particular person caught up in ignorance and forced to suffer its consequences.

Writing in expository lumps. An *expository lump* is an overly lengthy and detailed stretch of narration that provides extensive background or explains to the reader what is going on. Usually an expository lump merely *tells* readers what they should be *shown* instead. Consider this example: *Jim was referring to that fateful day when he and Martha were in medical school. Jim had wanted to be a doctor all his life, so the incident had been particularly painful to him. When he'd returned to his apartment after a long, hard day of classes, he'd found Martha sitting on the couch, crying . . . .*

In most cases, an expository lump should be replaced with scenes or stanzas that reveal the same information in a more dramatic and sensory manner. Sometimes the information in an expository lump can be revealed in bits and pieces throughout your piece, using narration, imagery and dialogue. And occasionally it makes the most sense to stick with a narrative explanation, but to shorten and simplify it greatly.

Having characters explain things to each other. This is simply an expository lump presented in dialogue form, e.g., "Well, Margot, as you know, we first took our jobs as cooks back in 1990, following that terrible accident in the elevator. After six months we started dating and eventually married. Today we work as chefs and live on Seventh Avenue. . . . " You can hear how ludicrous this sounds. Follow the advice immediately above.

Using stereotypes or caricatures. An important element of good writing is creating or revealing three-dimensional people. Resist the temptation to stereotype others, whether they're actual persons or fictional characters. Places can easily be stereotyped, too; when describing a setting, use more than just a few broad, familiar strokes.

Using antistereotypes. Don't fall into the trap of simply turning a portion of a stereotype upside down. When you show your reader a macho football player whose hobby is crocheting, or a mousy wallflower who likes to go big game hunting, you're still describing people two-dimensionally.

Failing to use standard American English. Don't use buzzwords or technical language unless you have good reason to, or unless you're sure your readers will understand what you mean. And if you write poetry, remember that poems aren't supposed to be written in some special poetic language that's high-handed, intellectual, Shakespearean or biblical. Like all forms of creative writing, poems should normally be written in standard American English. (Shakespeare's sonnets sound a bit formal to us now because they were written in the English of sixteenth- and seventeenth-century Britain.) You *can* alter standard American English occasionally in poetry — as well as in fiction and nonfiction — but only when you have good reason to, and only when standard language won't serve your purposes as well.

Overtly manipulating characters and/or events. Actually, it's fine to manipulate the characters and events in a work of fiction or poetry — but it's important that whatever happens *seems* natural and appropriate. Events should appear to evolve fluidly from previous occurrences, and characters should behave in ways that genuinely suit their personalities. Do your directing from off-stage, as subtly and invisibly as possible. If your reader can clearly see you pulling strings — i.e., if what happens in your piece doesn't feel intrinsic to the people and/or situations you've created — your piece will lose much of its impact; indeed, your reader may feel just as manipulated as the events and characters in it. Rethink your plot, and come up with a more subtle or believable sequence of events—or more believable reasons why your characters act as they do.

Stretching your reader's credulity. Your reader must accept the reality of what you write—if not literally, at least emotionally. When you play with your readers' sense of reality, do it in a way they'll find emotionally believable. If you discover yourself asking your reader to make too big a conceptual or emotional leap, replot your piece, or make that leap smaller, subtler or easier to handle.

Showing off. Don't try to impress your reader with your cleverness, cuteness or profundity. Your purpose as a writer is to move your readers, not to convince them of your ability or sensitivity. If something that genuinely fits well in your piece happens to be clever, cute or profound, by all means use it. But if it isn't necessary or important to your piece, then no matter how clever or profound it may be, it will only distract or disorient your reader. Get rid of it. (But don't throw it away; file it somewhere, or save it in your notebook. You'll probably be able to use it in a different piece.)

One further point: If something can be done simply, do it simply. Don't make it unnecessarily complex, especially if the only point of the complexity is to flaunt your skills or insight. As Philip Roth pointed out, writers often must work hard to make their writing look as if it came easily.

Being deliberately obscure or confusing. If you think confusion and obscurity are desirable—and some new writers think they are, particularly in poetry—please think again. Being unclear won't wow your readers with your brilliance; it will only leave them puzzled. (It's okay, of course, for a character to be confused, or for you to use confusion or obscurity to set up a mystery—provided that you adequately resolve this mystery.)

Rhyming unnecessarily. About 90 percent of poetry being published today makes little or no use of rhyme. Nevertheless, rhyming remains as useful, dynamic and creative a poetic device as ever. Like any poetic device, however, rhyme should be used only when it is intrinsic to your poem or genuinely adds to it. Using rhyme arbitrarily can undercut the impact of your poem, or make it seem forced or silly. Don't assume that rhyme is necessary just because you're writing a poem. And if you've started off rhyming and the piece doesn't seem to work, it may be best to drop the rhyme altogether—at least in your first draft. After the initial draft is complete, you can go back and, if appropriate, meld rhyme back in.

Overaccentuating rhyme, or using it as your sole poetic device. It is *not* true that if you're writing a poem, rhyme is all you need—any more than if you're writing dialogue, all you need are quotation marks. Rhyme is only one of many poetic devices. (See Step 25 for descriptions of many of these devices.) If you find yourself focusing almost exclusively on rhyme, refocus your attention on meaning, clarity and word choice, and make rhyme your fourth rather than first consideration.

Writing in greeting card language. This can take several forms: insipid poetry based on clichés and platitudes ("A friend is a gift"); deliberate but unnecessary overemphasis ("I was so jealous I could have *died*"); substituting syrup for real emotion ("When she thought about Clark, Marla's heart pounded inside her like the urgent beat of a savage's drum"); and, particularly in material for children, gross cutification (" 'Gosh,' thought Stripey the Tiger, 'I wonder if I could learn to sing all those nifty songs like Beaky the Bird' "). Greeting card writing is based on stock ideas and images rather than your own genuine interests, concerns and emotions. If you produce this kind of writing, look back at your responses to Step 7 once again, and bring your focus back to what's genuinely important to you.

Using clichés. A *cliché* is anything trite and overused. Clichés are usually phrases ("Look out for number one," "It's your funeral"), but they can also be images (a cheery soda jerk with a pointed white hat; a cat pawing at a ball of yarn), ideas (war is hell; Californians are laid-back), or even whole scenes (the soldier comes home from the war; the lovers wake up to a magnificent sunrise). When you notice yourself writing a cliché, replace it with something fresh—or transform it using a twist, embellishment or additional element. Use the tips in Steps 12 through 15 as guides.

Basing your piece on references to literature or art. New writers sometimes think this is classy, clever, articulate or profound—but it's usually just dull. Loading up your piece with literary or intellectual allusions won't move your readers, even if they recognize all of them. Allusions alone don't make for successful writing any more than nice-looking menus make for good restaurants. Look for meaning *within* your piece—in your people, events, images, observations and ideas. If you catch yourself focusing on other people's work or ideas, reorient your piece to what's important and meaningful to *you*. (Certain types of writing — e.g., reviews, parody and literary criticism — are obvious exceptions. These pieces *should*, of course, focus on the work and thought of others.)

Using vague language. Keep your language clear, specific and concrete. "Janine was dressed differently" doesn't create much of a mental picture. But "Janine had taken off her jumpsuit and was now dressed only in a blue bikini and sandals" offers the reader a strong, vivid image.

Inadvertently changing your viewpoint, tone or tense. It's perfectly legitimate to change any or all of these. But if you find that one of them has changed without your conscious direction, take careful note. Your unconscious has probably changed it into the best and most appropriate viewpoint, tone or tense for your piece (or at least for that part of it).

Using passive language. Some examples of passive language: "Delivery was completed." "The message was received." "The changing of management is being accomplished." In passive language, nobody performs actions; actions simply get performed. Passive language usually sounds stiff, distant, weak and bureaucratic.

Standard spoken and written English, on the other hand, is usually quite active. In standard American English, people *do* things. Some examples: "I delivered the wood." "Sue got the message." "Our management's changing. Frank quit, and Marguerite's replacing him." Each of these sentences is clear, concise and straightforward.

If you slip into passive language, translate the last passive sentence that you wrote into active language. Start with your subject, and follow it immediately with a clear, simple, straightforward verb. Then keep writing in the active mode.

Using other people's characters or ideas. Unless you've been specifically authorized to borrow from others, *don't*. If you catch yourself borrowing extensively, write that part of your piece again, this time drawing strictly from your own ideas, emotions, observations and concerns. (It is usually okay to use *brief* passages, concepts and quotations from others as examples in your work, so long as you credit the original authors. Indeed, I've done this several times in this book. However, any characters, fundamental points or central ideas should be your own.)

Confusing automatic writing with free verse or stream of consciousness. You may have heard of a writing technique called *free writing* or *automatic writing*, which involves writing in a steady stream whatever comes into your head. This is a perfectly legitimate method for getting words out onto the page (or the computer screen). However, it rarely creates a viable first draft. More often it results in a kind of prefirst draft — a set of images, lines and working notes not unlike what you came up with in Step 7. This material can help you create an initial draft and/or can be incorporated into it.

Beginning writers sometimes confuse free writing with free verse or stream of consciousness, which are very different. *Free verse* is poetry written without regular rhyme or meter. Good free verse is nevertheless quite carefully structured, and it makes use of a variety of poetic techniques. *Stream of consciousness* is the representation of a person's thoughts in prose or poetry; it, too, is usually carefully written and structured. Stream of consciousness can employ standard English (as in Nicholson Baker's *The Mezzanine*), or a kind of modified and somewhat ungrammatical English meant to imitate the direct flow of thoughts (as in William Faulkner's *The Sound and the Fury*).

YOUR ASSIGNMENT

As you work on your first draft, keep the pitfalls described above in the back of your mind. (If you don't consciously remember them all, that's fine, so long as you've read everything in this step carefully.)

If you sense that you're falling (or have already fallen) into one of these traps, read the appropriate advice in this step again. Then apply it to what you've just written, or to what you write next.

Important: You don't *have* to fix each problem as you notice it. If you can make a change easily, without breaking your writing momentum, that's great. But if you catch yourself, say, using vague language and clichés, it's fine to simply circle the passages in question, write a note to yourself about it (e.g., "vague & cliché — fix") and continue pressing ahead. Once your first draft is done, you can always return to those passages and work on them further.

PART THREE

Getting Your Work Into Shape

Look Over Your Work

Take a bow. You've done something that many people who desire to write never actually do: You've written a complete draft of a story, poem or essay.

This is a significant accomplishment—one that required vision, energy and persistence. These are the same attributes that you'll use to bring your piece to completion in the following four steps.

YOUR ASSIGNMENT

Strange as it may sound, your immediate task is to temporarily turn your attention to something *other* than your piece. In order to reread your finished draft with a fresh perspective and a clear mind, you'll need to distance yourself from it briefly. Spending some time away from your piece also gives your unconscious mind a chance to digest what you've done so far.

Most writers find it sufficient to put aside what they've written for a few hours, or (more commonly) overnight. Others may need two or three days, or even a week. As you gain writing experience, you'll soon get a feel for how long you typically need to be away from a draft in order to see it through fresh eyes. (The length of this interval can of course vary from piece to piece or draft to draft.)

It helps to deliberately refocus your energy. So take in a movie, read a book, go fishing, catch up on correspondence—or work on a different piece.

Once you've gotten some distance from your first draft, make yourself comfortable and begin rereading it—*aloud*. Do this slowly, seeing and hearing each word. Reading aloud enables you to absorb your piece through two different senses at once, thus doubling your perception and concentration.

Keep the following questions in mind as you read:

- What is this piece trying to do? (There may be more than one answer to this question.)
- Does the piece *generally* succeed at what it is trying to do?
- Which parts or passages are generally successful? Which are not?

If something looks, sounds and feels right as you read it, leave it alone — it's probably working well. But if your eyes, ears or feelings aren't comfortable with a certain passage, it probably needs more work. Make a note to come back to it.

Keep your original notes from Step 7 handy as you read your draft, and refer to them as necessary. If you prepared an outline or netline for your piece, keep this nearby as well.

Please don't make any changes, even obvious ones, in your manuscript just yet. Simply indicate which portions or passages need attention, and in each case note what the problem is (e.g., "dialogue seems too formal"). When you rewrite and revise in Step 18, you'll return to these passages and work on them.

As you read, also indicate gaps where things may need to be added, and cross out material that feels unnecessary or irrelevant.

If you feel that parts of your piece may need to be rearranged, make a note to this effect (e.g., "place after third stanza," or draw arrows). If you're not sure which order the various sections should go in, simply write "reorder" in the appropriate spot(s), and keep reading. During Step 18 you'll be able to work further on the structure of your piece.

Ignore errors in spelling, punctuation and grammar for now. At this stage, these errors are irrelevant, since you will likely rewrite significant portions of your piece. You'll have a chance to deal with these small details in Step 19.

As you read through your draft, pay special attention to any images, ideas, observations, dialogue, metaphors, descriptions and other items that you feel work well. I suggest underlining each such passage and writing "good" next to it. This is important, because it demonstrates at a glance the strong points of your first draft. When you rewrite and revise in Step 18, these positive comments will help you decide which material to keep in. Furthermore, being able to see what you've done well will help inspire you.

Once you've finished reading through your draft and making

notes, take a break. (This can be as brief as ten minutes or as long as a couple of days; the choice is yours.) Then go back and reread aloud your entire first draft again. This is important, because your ear will often notice and reveal things to you that your eyes may have missed.

Go slowly and take your time, just as before. Also as before, make notes on what works and what doesn't. This time, though, also jot down what you think can be done to fix each problem (e.g., "relocate scene to shopping center," "find less obvious metaphor," etc.).

As you reread your draft for the second time, be on the lookout for some of the common writing problems described in Step 16. (You may wish to review that step briefly.) If you notice your piece falling into one of those traps, write a note at the appropriate spot.

Chances are good that on this second round you'll notice things about your draft that you didn't catch the first time. By all means write down these observations. If you find yourself disagreeing with a note that you wrote when you first reread your draft, place a question mark above your previous comment. You'll have a chance to consider the passage further in Step 18.

Don't worry if critiquing your own work seems difficult at first, or if you're not quite sure what to look for or write down. Critiquing your work is a pragmatic, seat-of-the-pants process; there aren't any absolute rules or procedures to follow. Simply feel your way and use your eyes, ears, gut and best judgment. As you become more experienced at writing, rereading and rewriting, you'll get steadily better at knowing what works, what doesn't, and what needs to be done next.

When you've finished this step, you'll be ready—and well-prepared—to do some more writing.

Rewrite Your Piece

To *rewrite* or *revise* your piece simply means to make significant changes in it.

Most writers must do quite a bit of rewriting, revising or revision (the terms are synonymous), as well as some careful editing and proofreading, before they consider a piece finished. This is at least as true for experienced writers as it is for beginners. Indeed, this very chapter went through five drafts and a great deal of line-by-line editing before I felt it was done.

Editing is the act of fine-tuning a piece—attending to its small points and smoothing out its rough edges. This means correcting word choice, punctuation, sentence structure, grammar, factual references and other minor items. Editing should begin only after the process of revision is complete.

Proofreading is the process of checking for technical problems, such as missing words, misspellings, typographical errors and so on. There is of course little point in proofreading a piece until it has been fully edited. (I'll discuss editing and proofreading in greater detail in Step 19.)

Revising and editing are fundamentally different processes, and you can't substitute one for the other. A piece with a flawed central premise, for example, can't be fixed by any amount of editing; it needs to be rethought and rewritten.

When you rewrite a piece, you may or may not complete additional *drafts* or *revisions*, which are new versions of your piece written more or less from beginning to end. Many writers find that they revise most effectively by writing a complete second draft, then a third, and then (if necessary) a fourth, until their piece does what they want it to do. They'll keep their previous drafts close at hand, and as they write each new draft they'll incorporate the best passages and sections from those earlier versions. Thus most of their revisions combine both new and old material.

Not everyone revises in such a linear, draft-by-draft fashion, however. Some writers prefer to focus on one section, scene or stanza at a time, going over that section repeatedly until they're happy with it, then moving on to another. (They needn't do this sequentially; they might, for example, work first on their ending, then on their beginning, and so on.)

The late fiction writer Sara Vogan used to rewrite by focusing on one specific aspect of a piece at a time. After writing her first or second draft, she'd go through it to get the central metaphor working correctly; then she'd go through it again, focusing on dialogue; then she'd work with imagery and settings, then with pacing, and so on.

There are yet other ways to revise productively. Some writers like to produce alternate versions of the same section or piece. For example, they might write four versions of the same poem, each from the point of view of a different character. Or they might write a dozen different scenes involving the same three people; then they'll choose the scenes that seem the most promising and build a short story around them. Or they'll start with a central premise and deliberately take it in several different directions, then work with the direction that most appeals to them.

Still other writers use a combination of techniques, tailoring the revision process to suit the particular piece and circumstances. For example, they might find themselves *redrafting* (writing new drafts of) certain portions of their piece, but leaving other sections largely intact. Then they might create an interim outline or netline, then change the order in which the sections of their piece appear, then redraft some troublesome passages once again, and so on, until they feel their piece is ready for editing.

In short, *there is no one right way to rewrite.* Furthermore, since you don't have to write and rewrite in successive drafts, there is no "right" number of drafts that you should expect to complete. Each piece is different. The first piece that you write might require three full drafts and lots of section-by-section work; the next might emerge in first draft in near-finished shape, requiring nothing more than some snatches of rewriting here and there; your third might need half a dozen full rewrites, plus additional close work on many sections and passages; and your fourth might require almost no revision in its initial sections, but a great deal in the rest. (Eudora Welty said that her stories typically required dozens of revisions; Samuel Beckett, on the other hand, claimed that much of his work came out full-blown in a single draft.)

You're finished rewriting when your piece's significant elements—its themes, ideas, central images or metaphors, pacing, characterization, tone, settings, dialogue, etc.—all work well, fit together and generally feel right. In short, you can move on to editing when your piece consistently does what you want it to do—even though it may still have rough spots.

YOUR ASSIGNMENT

Put in front of you everything you've written on your piece so far: your notes from Step 7, your outline or netline (if you have one), your writer's notebook and your first draft. Place the draft in the most visible and convenient spot. Keep a thesaurus nearby.

Now begin revising what you've written. Refer to any or all of the above materials as you wish. Here are some tips that will help you rewrite:

1. Start by focusing on the largest concerns, such as your central character, premise, point, metaphor, image, plot or theme. *After* you've got these major items working, look at slightly less central concerns, such as overall structure, pacing, dialogue, tone, secondary images and metaphors, and so on. (There's no point in tinkering with your dialogue, for instance, when you need to completely replot your piece or rethink one of its major characters.)

2. Don't fiddle with grammar, punctuation, spelling or other small details. Dealing with these while revising can distract you from your piece's more serious problems. Furthermore, editing during the revision process is often pointless, since you might need to rewrite what you've just edited.

3. Let your piece go where it wants to go. New ideas, images and directions may reveal themselves to you as you revise. Neither accept nor reject any such possibility automatically, but evaluate each one on a case-by-case basis. If something feels right, be willing to use it, even if it means abandoning your original outline or intention. If this new approach ultimately doesn't work, return to your original plan.

4. In revision, sustaining your momentum is not as important as

it is when writing a first draft. If you get sidetracked or stuck, it's okay to stop and mull over the situation.

5. When you begin revising, your piece may seem awkward, misshapen or downright awful. This is quite common for early drafts, so take heart. As you rewrite, your piece will steadily come into focus and take shape. If a successful finished piece were represented by a perfect circle, your piece might look like the illustration below as you revise and edit it:

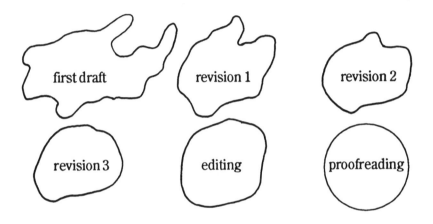

6. Before you begin any new draft—or when you begin each new rewriting session—read aloud what you've done so far, slowly, letting your ears and eyes absorb the words. This will help you to orient yourself and see and hear things that you may have missed before.

7. Whenever you make a change, read it aloud a few times to see if it looks and sounds right. If it doesn't, that passage probably requires further attention. Similarly, if you have trouble with a particular passage or section, read it aloud an extra time or two, looking and listening carefully. Sometimes your ear will pick up clues that your eye has missed.

8. Many (but by no means all) writers feel that it's a good idea to take a break after each round of revision. This interval helps them clear their minds and bring a fresh perspective to their piece each time they return to it. Depending on the writer, this break might last a few hours, overnight, or a couple of days.

9. One of the most important aspects of revising is *cutting*—get-

ting rid of things that your piece doesn't need. These can be individual words or phrases; entire scenes, stanzas or sections; or anything in between. Painful though it may be at first, cutting is an absolutely essential skill. Here are some things to keep in mind:

- There's an amazing amount of fat and repetition in virtually every essay, poem or story in progress—so plan to do a good deal (or even a great deal) of cutting, no matter what you're writing. Furthermore, expect to make additional cuts each time you reread what you've written. When James M. Cain revised his novel *The Postman Always Rings Twice*, he ended up cutting more than half of what he'd written.

- Cut anything that isn't genuinely useful to your piece; anything that doesn't support what your piece (or the appropriate portion of it) is trying to do; anything that does your piece more harm than good; and anything that isn't worth the number of words it requires.

- If you're unsure whether to leave something in, reread that section of your piece aloud. Do this twice—once with the passage in question included, and once without it. This should help you decide which route to take. If you still can't decide, however, it's probably best to cut the material. As the old writing adage goes, "When in doubt, leave it out."

- If you can't get a passage or section to work right no matter what you do, consider cutting it entirely. Usually this will solve the problem.

- Cutting doesn't just mean eliminating items. Sometimes it means combining or simplifying different elements or passages. For instance, you might reduce a wordy paragraph to a sentence or two; shorten a lengthy description to a couple of important details; compress two or three phrases into one; or replace a stretch of narrative (or even an entire scene) with a simple statement or transition, such as "Later, at the police station," or "That night, however, things went just as Kim had predicted."

- Occasionally something may strike you as interesting, insightful or even brilliant—but it doesn't fit into your piece. In such cases, *always* cut it. If something doesn't belong, it doesn't belong, no matter how wonderful it may be. Put it in your writer's notebook or some other accessible spot, and save it for use in some other piece.

10. Throughout the revision process, your guiding principles should continue to be, "What moves, intrigues or fascinates me?" and "What do I want to say, do, see or have happen in this piece?" If you find yourself lost, stuck or at a crossroads, ask yourself these questions again. If you remain stuck, open your notebook and look through it carefully. You'll probably find something in it to add to your piece — or redirect it — that will get it moving again. If even this doesn't work, however, try the strategies for getting unstuck that I discuss in Step 11.)

11. Don't show your story, poem or essay to anyone while you're revising it. Getting feedback from others while you're still rewriting and envisioning your piece can short-circuit your creative process. Get your piece in the best shape you can first; *then* bring it to someone you trust for an evaluation. (One exception: If you find yourself utterly stuck and unable to proceed any further on your own — even after you've looked through your writer's notebook and tried the suggestions in Step 11 — advice and criticism from someone else may help get your piece moving again.) Step 21 will deal with the process of getting useful feedback from others.

12. Occasionally, despite your best efforts, a piece simply might not come together for you. If, after several rounds of revision, your piece seems to go nowhere — or if you simply lose interest in it — your best bet may be to abandon it. (But save everything you've written; you might be able to use it later.) Look again at your responses to the first two parts of Step 7. Use these to develop a set of working notes for a new piece; then write a first draft for this piece by following the guidelines in Steps 9-16. Once you've finished this initial draft, use the tips in Steps 17-18 to help you reread and revise this new piece.

This step can take a good deal of time, so don't rush through it. Revise your piece as much as you need to, keeping in mind that each time you go through it, you bring it one important notch closer to completion.

Edit and Proofread

E*diting* (sometimes called *polishing*) is the process of adjusting and fine-tuning your piece. It's the literary equivalent of adjusting the timing on your car, tossing a salad, or sanding and painting a bookcase you've just built.

As in rewriting, when you edit you'll add, replace, rearrange and cut material. Editing functions on a much smaller scale, however. It focuses primarily on individual words, phrases, lines and sentences, and only rarely on full stanzas or paragraphs. It also involves checking grammar, usage, punctuation, spelling and stylistic unity (e.g., capitalizing the first word of every line in a poem, or beginning each new section with an italicized heading).

You can begin editing only when you're done revising or rethinking your piece. If you have not yet reached this point, your piece needs further revision.

A poem, essay or story that generally works well and needs no more revising may nevertheless require a great deal of editing. Occasionally a piece may even need little or no rewriting at all, but lots of close line-by-line editing. Indeed, several chapters in this book were written in only one or two drafts but required up to a dozen rounds of editing.

As you edit, pay close attention to rhythm, pacing, word choice, accuracy (if appropriate), and sentence and paragraph structure. In addition, consider your choice and presentation of each detail, image and metaphor. If your piece is a poem, also examine line and stanza breaks, physical layout and appearance, and sound devices such as alliteration, assonance, consonance and onomatopoeia. I'll define these sound devices, and others, in Step 25.

With few exceptions, works in progress require several rounds of editing. It simply isn't possible to catch and correct everything in a single read-through. In fact, you'll probably find that you can edit your piece half a dozen times or more, and each time see or hear problems you missed.

When your piece is as strong, as successful and as polished as you can make it, it's ready for *proofreading* (sometimes called *proofing*). Unlike rewriting and editing, proofreading is essentially a technical rather than a creative task. It's your final check to make sure that everything in your piece is complete and correct. This includes punctuation, grammar, capitalization, spelling, typing, page setup, spacing, typefaces and fonts (e.g., italics, bold, etc.) and so on. When you proofread, you take a last look to make sure that everything in your piece does exactly what you want it to.

YOUR ASSIGNMENT

Reread your piece carefully — slowly and aloud. Make any necessary changes, cuts and additions. After you make each change, read the edited passage aloud a couple of times to make sure it looks and sounds right. If it doesn't, keep working on it.

When you've gone all the way through your piece, repeat the process to catch things you missed the first time. I can all but promise there will be plenty of such items. If necessary, go back and edit it a third time — and, if need be, a fourth and a fifth. Do as many rounds of editing as your piece requires.

It is not normally necessary to take a break in between rounds — but if you wish to or feel it might be helpful, by all means do so.

Continue editing until your piece is as effective and well formed as you can get it to be. Keep the following guidelines in mind:

• Keep your early drafts, original notes, outline or netline (if any) and writer's notebook nearby. Refer back to these as you need to, especially if you have trouble finding the right word, image, phrase or detail. One of these resources may provide you with just what you need — or inspire you to come up with it on your own.

• For many writers, a thesaurus can be absolutely invaluable during editing; keep yours handy. When I edit my work, I probably refer to my thesaurus at least three times an hour. (Don't, however, use a thesaurus that's built into word processing software; most of these electronic variations are inaccurate and have few entries.)

• Cutting is as essential to editing as it is to revision. Be on the lookout for words, phrases, sentences and lines that are unnecessary, or that are longer or more complex than they need to be. Be prepared to simplify, condense and excise passages. Though it's unusual at this point, you may even need to simplify or get rid of entire paragraphs, stanzas, scenes or sections. Remember to save anything that's interesting, moving or amusing for possible use in another piece. Either put it in your notebook or place it in a separate file.

• Watch for—and fix—words and phrases that are vague, unclear, confusing, clichéd or unintentionally (and detrimentally) ambiguous.

• Make sure that any changes you made during revision are consistent throughout your piece. For instance, if you've changed a character's name from Marlene to Marian, make sure that she's referred to as Marian at all times. And if you've changed the time of year from December to July, make sure that you've rewritten the paragraph in which Marian looks out the window at the falling snow.

• If you're not sure which word is best, which form of punctuation is appropriate, which rule of grammar or usage applies (or how to apply it), or how a certain word is spelled, don't guess—look it up. For checking grammar, usage or punctuation, I recommend *Hodges' Harbrace College Handbook* (Harcourt Brace), which is inexpensive and easy to use, and *The Gregg Reference Manual* by William A. Sabin (Glencoe/McGraw-Hill). Check definitions in your dictionary or thesaurus. To check spellings, use your dictionary, your thesaurus, or the spell-checking feature of your word processor or word processing program. Another option is a spelling dictionary—a slim, inexpensive book that lists the correct spellings (but no definitions) of most English words. If spelling is a particular problem for you, I also suggest buying a very helpful volume called *The Bad Speller's Dictionary* (Random House), which lists words alphabetically by their most common misspellings.

• Some computer programs are supposedly capable of editing, checking grammar and punctuation, analyzing your style, and even critiquing your work for you. Do not use these programs or features, however, because none does an even marginally acceptable job. Indeed, some of them may even damage your piece or distort your natural style by applying hard-and-fast rules to a language that is by nature quirky and fluid.

You'll know that the editing process is winding down when the number of changes you make in each cycle of editing has begun to diminish. You're ready to begin proofing when, for two rounds of editing in a row, you make no more than a few small corrections each time. (Don't worry about those few changes. You've simply reached the point of diminishing returns, where no matter how many times you reread your piece, you'll probably find a couple of tiny changes to make each time. It's important not to get stuck here; tell yourself that you'll have a chance to catch any problems as you proofread, and move on.)

You're ready to move from editing to proofreading when your piece does what you want it to, sounds right when read aloud, looks right on the page, and feels right to you as well.

It's important not to let your eagerness to finish—or simple impatience or weariness—push you into declaring your piece ready for proofreading prematurely. Do what needs to be done—no less, and no more.

Like revising, proofreading is best done slowly and aloud. Use your ears as well as your eyes, so that one sense can catch what the other might miss.

I suggest proofreading your piece twice. Or, if you like, proof it once yourself and then have someone else proof it; often a second pair of eyes will notice things that the first pair overlooked. Feel free to use a spell-checking program if you like, but only in addition to two full rounds of proofing by an alert, intelligent human being.

If the second time you proofread your piece you still find a significant number of items that need to be corrected, proof it a third time. Repeat this process until you can read your piece from beginning to end without finding a single problem.

Don't plan on editing as you proofread. Nevertheless, if you *do* spot something that needs attention, by all means work on it until you feel you've gotten it right.

Some writers, once they've finished proofreading their work, like to put it aside for a while—anywhere from a few days to a week or two. Then they'll read it over again with (ideally, at least) a fresh perspective—and, if necessary, edit and proofread it further. This strategy isn't a required part of this step, but it is a potentially useful option. Remember that you always have the right to work further on any piece you've written—even if you previously declared it finished.

Find the Right Title

N o essay, story or poem is complete without a title. And not just any title, but the *right* title.

Sometimes the perfect title for your piece may leap out at you, or be so obvious that you scarcely need to think about it. In some cases, you might even know what your title is before you start writing; it's even possible to start out with only a title, which in turn will provide you with the inspiration or ideas for creating your piece.

For other pieces, your title may prove more elusive — or it may emerge only with care and patience, as the result of conscious and deliberate effort.

A title must genuinely *add* something to a piece, rather than merely restate it, describe it, or sum it up in some general way. (Would you have picked up this book if it were called *How to Write* or *A Book for New Writers?*) A good title gives your reader a new (or wider) perspective, an extra thought or image, a twist, an irony, a bisociation, an additional metaphor, an added emphasis, or some moving or thought-provoking counterpoint. Still more important, it does this in a way that deepens or strengthens the piece.

When considering a particular title, ask yourself if your reader will get more out of your piece with that title than without it. If the answer is yes, you're onto something; if it's no, the title simply won't do the job.

Some of the best titles are effective in two entirely different ways. Before you begin reading the piece, the title draws you in and prepares you subliminally for what you're about to read. Then, when you've finished reading and look back at the title, it resonates in another very different way.

Joan Didion's essay, "Some Dreamers of the Golden Dream," is an excellent example. It initially appears to be about idealistic people who resettle in California — the Golden State — where they hope to fulfill their dreams of a better life. By the time you've finished this grim and disturbing essay, however, the title has taken on entirely new meaning. It has become clear that Didion's California dreamers are out of touch with reality. They inhabit a mental world of movies, newspapers, violence and greed; their dreams are psychotic fantasies. After you've read this essay, it's evident that the word *golden* in the title is heavily laden with irony, if not outright sarcasm.

Many good titles are deliberately catchy — e.g., Grace Paley's *Enormous Changes at the Last Minute*, Bill McKibben's *The End of Nature*, Harold Kushner's *When Bad Things Happen to Good People*, and Nathaniel Hawthorne's *The Celestial Railroad*. But catchiness isn't a necessity. Sometimes, in fact, a simple, restrained, understated title can be quite powerful, precisely because the piece it accompanies is anything *but* restrained or understated. Perhaps the best example of this is Shirley Jackson's "The Lottery." This brief story, written in a straightforward, almost journalistic style, details an annual small-town lottery. At first everything seems quite routine and commonplace, but as the story proceeds, the situation becomes steadily more ominous, and eventually terrifying.

Good titles can also be ironic, as in Gwendolyn Brooks's "We Real Cool." This short poem, written (in 1960) in poetic syncopation, is narrated by a Harlem jazz musician and pool shooter. He describes his and his cronies' lives in a total of eight lines, beginning with "we real cool" — but by line eight we've come to think of him as anything *but* cool. Indeed, our reaction is wholehearted pity.

Sometimes a title can be powerful and affecting because it can be read in two different ways at once, such as Eric Bogosian's *Drinking in America* or Alan Watts's *In My Own Way*. The further one reads in either of these fine books, the more the book resonates in both of the ways implied by its title.

Often a line, phrase or quotation from your piece can serve as an excellent title, as in Flannery O'Connor's "A Good Man Is Hard to Find," or the film *Lilies of the Field*. A title can also highlight a significant image or metaphor from your piece — as in, for instance, Sylvia Plath's *The Bell Jar*, Jerzy Kosinski's *The Painted Bird*, or Dylan Thomas's "The Peaches." (The title of Thomas's story seems quite flat at first, but it takes on a great deal of meaning by the end of the piece.) It's also possible to draw a good title from an idea, setting, character, or virtually any other element of your piece.

Actually, the art of composing titles hasn't been practiced as well as it could have been over the years. A surprising number of good works of literature — as well as innumerable not-so-good ones — have dull, simplistic or inappropriate titles. For example, Poe's "The Raven" and Jorge Luis Borges's *Ficciones* (Spanish for *Fictions*), though both first-rate, bear extraordinarily lackluster titles.

The bottom line is this: Your title is how people will remember your piece. So why not make it worth remembering?

YOUR ASSIGNMENT

Write a title for your piece — not just a good or appropriate one, but the best and most appropriate title you can imagine.

If you already have a good idea what your title should be, wonderful. Jump down nine paragraphs and follow the instructions for fine-tuning and refining it.

If you're uncertain as yet what your title should be, or if you have no ideas for it at all, follow the guidelines immediately below.

First, place your proofread manuscript in front of you. Also keep your various drafts, your notes, your netline or outline (if any) and your writer's notebook nearby, so that you can refer to them as you please.

Read through your piece once more, at any pace you wish. This time around, though, you don't have to read it aloud. You don't even have to read every word; feel free to skim or to skip back and forth among the various sections. As you read, look for key lines, concepts, images, metaphors and bits of dialogue. If you like, write these down.

Meditate on your piece for several minutes. Let your mind wander among its various elements. If you like, look back through your early drafts and other material. See what clicks or connects, and write it down. Then work with these items until you've come up with a title that looks, sounds and feels right.

Here are a few cautions:

• Don't be clever or elaborate just to be clever or elaborate. If a title doesn't strengthen or deepen your piece in some way, it's not right. Save it in your notebook; you may be able to use it with some other piece.

• Avoid titles that are vague or general, or that could apply to almost any piece of literature (e.g., "The Journey," "An Encounter,"

"Growing," etc.). These are by nature ineffectual.

• Don't be too obvious or explanatory (e.g., "Jeremy's Sudden, Unexpected Suicide"). You don't want to telegraph a surprise ending, or give your readers so much information that they hardly need to read your piece at all.

In something as brief as a title, every word can make an important difference. Once you've got the right concept or focus for your title, you may still need to edit it to make it as strong and effective as possible. Consider all possible variations. You might need to choose the best form of a key word, or select just the right modifying words, or pick out precisely the right part of a pivotal phrase. For instance, once you're sure that your title will be brief and will center around the word *exhibition*, you may need to decide between "A Day at the Exhibition," "At the Exhibition" or simply "The Exhibition."

When you've got the right title for the piece, you'll know it.

And if you come up with an even better title later on, by all means use it.

Get Critical Feedback From Someone You Trust

O nce you've gotten your piece in the best shape you can, you're ready to show it to someone else. But not just anyone else—someone whose judgment you trust and respect.

If you're like many new writers, this may be the most anxiety-producing part of the whole writing process. You're making your piece—and yourself—vulnerable to someone else's opinions and judgments.

But learning to thoughtfully listen to, evaluate, accept and sometimes reject the judgments of others is an essential writing skill. Furthermore, feedback from someone you trust can help you see more clearly many of your piece's strengths *and* weaknesses, and notice others that you may have overlooked. It gives you a chance to test-market your piece, to get a sense (albeit a limited one) of how your readers may respond to it. And it provides you with an opportunity to improve your piece *before* you present it to the general public.

But what if your critic finds flaws in your piece, perhaps even serious ones? Then you've done exactly the right thing by getting their feedback. Using their most helpful comments as guides, you'll be able to strengthen your piece and fix any problems you may have missed.

Your ideal critic is someone who's intelligent, whom you trust and respect, who reads regularly, who is reasonably articulate, and who thinks much like you do. What's most important, though, is that they are sympathetic to the kind of piece you've written. If your piece is a mystery, don't give it to someone who doesn't care for mysteries; no matter how wonderful a critic they might otherwise be, they're not likely to give you very constructive feedback. Find someone who likes mysteries.

Your critic must be able to be honest with you. If they can't be (or if you suspect they can't), find someone else. This is a particular concern if you're thinking about getting feedback from a friend, relative or spouse.

Your critic should also have no agenda to push and no axe to grind. They need to be able to look at your piece on its own terms — to see (and, ideally, to appreciate) what it tries to do and to evaluate how well it does it.

Your critic should be specific and detailed about the various elements of your piece. Their comments should go well beyond "I liked it" or "I enjoyed the last several stanzas." They should be able to point to individual sections and passages and clearly discuss how they work — or how and why they don't.

Your critic doesn't have to be a writing instructor, a literature scholar, a published writer (or a writer at all) or a college graduate. They don't need to have a background in literature, though it certainly helps if they're widely read, particularly in your piece's genre.

Any of the following people may be a helpful critic:

- A like-minded and intelligent friend, colleague, relative or spouse — one who is genuinely able to be honest and (helpfully) critical of your work. This is usually your best bet.
- Another writer whose opinions (and, ideally, whose work) you respect.
- A writing instructor at a college, writers' center or other institution. (At some colleges, you may need to register for independent study to receive one-to-one criticism. You also may be eligible to receive academic credit. Most colleges charge for independent study.)
- An instructor at a writers' conference. (At many writers' conferences, workshops and retreats, manuscript criticism is included as part of the package; at others, critiques are available for an additional charge.)
- A writer-in-residence at a nearby library, writers' center, art center, community center or other community organization.
- A writing consultant or professional manuscript critic. (These professionals normally charge thirty to sixty-five dollars an

hour, though some charge by the page or piece. I charge fifty dollars per hour—slightly more than average.)

Some literary agents critique manuscripts in exchange for a (usually hefty) reading fee. I *strongly* recommend against paying any literary agent to read or critique your work. Agents are essentially sales representatives for writers; thus they tend to want every literary project to conform as closely as possible to whatever is selling well at the moment. Typically, an agent will respond unfavorably to a serious and ambitious literary project, but will give high praise to a glitzy but utterly predictable piece that's loaded down with lurid sex and violence.

I also advise against having your work criticized in a writers' group. Although some of these groups can be quite helpful, they're primarily for people with a good deal of writing experience. If you present your piece to such a group, you run the risk of having it torn to shreds by a mean-spirited group member. And if you join a beginners' group, you may receive criticism that's largely unfounded or wrongheaded. If a writer's group interests you, feel free to join one—but wait until you've completed at least six to ten pieces.

Ideally, you'll be able to find a good critic from among the people you know. If you need to look elsewhere, however, here are some suggestions:

- Call one or more of the following: the literature department of the main branch of any big-city library; the main office of the department of English, creative writing or journalism at a university or college; a nearby art center; the manager of a good bookstore (not a chain store, however); or the office of a writers' conference, workshop, studio or colony. Ask for the names and phone numbers of two or three professional manuscript critics.
- Contact one of the many writers' centers (also called literary centers) across North America. Many of these have working arrangements with manuscript critics. For example, The Loft, a writers' center in Minneapolis, publishes a booklet called "One on One," which describes the services of thirteen such critics. A good list of writers' centers appears in my book *1,818 Ways to Write Better & Get Published* (Writer's Digest Books).
- Ask your friends and/or any writers you know for suggestions.

- The National Writers Club (1450 South Havana, Suite 620, Aurora, CO 80012, (303) 751-7844) and *Writer's Digest* magazine (1507 Dana Avenue, Cincinnati, OH 45207, (513) 531-2222) both sponsor manuscript criticism services. Write or call for prices and other details.

Before you hire any professional critic, it's important to learn something about their background. How much experience have they had as a critic, writer, editor, writing consultant and/or writing teacher? What types of writing (e.g., essays, science fiction, children's books, poetry, etc.) do they specialize in or especially like? What do they charge? If you like, ask for one or two references. Only work with someone who sounds sharp and honest—and whom you feel good about.

Furthermore, before you get criticism from anyone, even a friend, ask them these questions:

- Are you interested in commercial writing, literary writing, or both?
- How do you generally feel about the genre in which my piece is written (e.g., poetry, mystery, fantasy, personal essay, etc.)?
- What types of writing do you dislike or find boring?
- Will you be honest and straightforward with me at all times?
- Will you point out both the weaknesses *and* the strengths of my piece?
- Will you not only show me where my piece needs work, but make specific suggestions for what I should do next?
- Will you consider my piece on its own terms, and base your critique on what it tries to do?
- What are your literary biases, if any?

Some critics prefer to provide a written critique; some prefer in-person meetings; still others work largely over the phone; and some critics, like me, vary or combine these arrangements, depending on the particular project and the needs of the writer. If you have a preference, clearly say so up front. Also, let your critic know of any particular concerns you have or items you want addressed. For example: "I'm especially interested in your reaction to the scenes set in Atlanta. Do they work? And does the piece need all of them, particularly the first one?"

Here is the single most important thing you need to know about receiving feedback on your work: You don't have to agree with your critic's evaluation or do what they suggest. And here's the second most important consideration: If you don't agree, don't try to defend your piece or argue the point. Criticism isn't a debate. It's not the critic's job to convince you of anything, nor is it yours to convince them. A good critic will simply present you with their best analysis, observations, insights and suggestions. It then is your task to listen alertly, take notes as appropriate, and consider carefully each of your critic's comments. If, after this careful thought, something makes sense to you, do it; if it doesn't, ignore it.

You may, however, explain what you were trying to do in a particular passage or section, and then ask, "Does it work? If not, why not? What do I need to do to make it work? Is what I'm trying to do worth doing at all?" Make sure you and your critic ask each other whatever additional pertinent questions come to mind.

Now for the third most important point about receiving feedback: *Never* do something to your piece that you don't agree with or believe in. Do what you feel is best, even if your critic is adamant that you need to do something else—and even if they've published forty books and won the Nobel Prize in literature. After all, it's possible to be absolutely certain about something and be wrong (I certainly have been). Furthermore, famous writers, literature professors, and even Nobel Prize winners can be just as fallible or shortsighted as anyone. Consider each comment you receive on its own merits, regardless of who made it. This applies to positive as well as negative comments.

Speaking of negative comments, these may hurt at first. But remember that these comments reflect only on your piece, which is still in progress—*not* on you as a person or on your ability as a writer. (If someone *does* say disparaging things about you or your overall writing ability, they're totally out of line. Find a different critic.) Also keep in mind that negative criticism will get much easier to hear and accept as you gain more writing experience.

Ultimately, only you can decide which advice to follow, which advice to ignore, and which changes (if any) to make in your piece. No matter what anyone else may think or say, ultimately every decision about your piece is yours and yours alone.

Will you always know which advice to follow and which advice to ignore? No. Will you always make the right decision? No again. But you *will* get better at both with practice and experience. And because writing is not like performing a flute sonata, you don't have to present your piece publicly until you feel it's ready. If at any point you realize that your piece needs further changes, or that something you previously disagreed with makes sense after all, simply revise your piece once again.

The guidelines in this step should help you find a useful and effective critic. Nevertheless, since there are some second-rate (and even abusive) critics around, it's helpful to know which kinds of critical comments are *not* valid. Watch out for the following:

- Anything expressed as an absolute—e.g., "All writers must write only from their own experience" or "All mysteries must start out with a problem or question."
- Anything that makes a judgment about you as a person—e.g., "From the looks of this piece, you don't deserve serious criticism" or "Only a crazy person could have written this."
- Anything that reflects negatively on your writing ability as a whole—e.g., "You don't have the stuff to be a writer" or "You should stick to writing short stories, because you don't have much talent as an essayist." Your critic has neither the evidence nor the right to make such a sweeping judgment.
- Any appeal to authority that is meant to supersede your own best judgment—e.g., "Well, the editor of *The Paris Review* said exactly the same thing, and if anybody should know, it's him."
- Any negative comment about your work paired with a self-compliment—e.g., "Your dialogue doesn't sound real here, and believe me, I know, because I'm a dialogue expert." Your critic's real agenda may be to praise themselves rather than to help you.
- Anything that doesn't deal specifically with your piece—e.g., "Back in the '60s we used to sit around the Triangle Bar and think up ideas like these, just for fun; it was a lot more interesting to be a writer in those days."
- Anything that's vague or ambiguous—e.g., "I think you need to reformat this," or "There's something missing in this piece's texture." Ask for—and, if necessary, insist on—clarification.

If you'd like to get critical feedback from more than one person, feel free. Indeed, a second critic may notice things that your first critic doesn't and/or provide additional fresh insights or perspectives. But any two critics will rarely completely agree, regardless of what they critique. They'll almost certainly disagree on some small things, and perhaps on some large ones as well. Experiencing such disagreement first-hand can help you quickly get used to hearing, sorting out and weighing differing opinions, then coming to your own conclusion. On the other hand, such overt disagreement can sometimes be quite confusing, particularly to new writers.

If you decide to get feedback from more than one person, *never* try to play one critic against the other. For instance, don't say to critic B, "It's interesting that you think this section doesn't work, because critic A really liked it." Neither critic will feel good about this. Listen to each person's comments carefully and thoughtfully; if need be, ask for clarification and details. Then make your own best decision.

YOUR ASSIGNMENT

First, ask yourself whom you know who might be able to give you useful feedback on your piece. Make a list of these names. Speak with each person briefly; if they're interested in reading and critiquing your piece, ask them the questions on page 93. Keep in mind that you want someone who reads and enjoys the type of piece you've written, who can be honest with you, whose opinion you value, and whom you feel you can trust.

If you can't find a good critic among the people you already know, follow the guidelines earlier in this step to find a talented and reliable professional.

If you want to show your piece to two different people, or even three, that's fine. For the purposes of this step, however, make three your maximum.

As you get feedback, listen carefully, and take notes if you need to. Don't argue or defend your piece. When you've gotten all of each critic's comments, thank them for their help.

Spend some time looking and thinking over all of the feedback you've gotten. Consider each comment on its own merits. Be thorough, thoughtful and careful. Decide which comments and suggestions genuinely apply to your piece and which ones do not.

Repeat Steps 17-19, rereading, revising, editing and proofreading your piece as necessary. Don't be surprised if this time around the process goes more smoothly. (If, once you've done this, you still have concerns or doubts about your piece, you have the option of getting further feedback on it, and then doing additional revision, editing and proofing as necessary.)

When you've completed all this, your piece is finished.

You've accomplished a great deal so far. You've not only gotten started as a writer, but you've gone through every step of the writing process from beginning to end. Furthermore, you've created a full, polished, finished piece — and you've proven to yourself that you can do it.

Give yourself a big hand.

What should you do with your piece now that it's finished? Anything you like. Give copies to friends, relatives and acquaintances. If you wish, try to get it published by following the guidelines in Steps 26-28. Or, for the time being, simply file it away and move on to the following step. (Always save every piece you write, by the way — for as long as you live. You never know when you'll want to reread it, revise it or try to publish it — perhaps even years or decades from now.)

Everything you've done in the first twenty-one steps has served you well. Now that you've completed these steps, you have all the tools, talents and experience you need to write a complete story, essay or poem whenever you want to.

Turn to Part Four and you'll put your tools, talents and experience to good use once again.

Getting More Experienced

Finish Several Pieces

I n writing, as in so many other things, there's no substitute for hands-on experience, and no better method for learning and growing. The more writing practice you get, the better and more confident a writer you're likely to become.

You learned to write a finished essay, story or poem by actually writing one from beginning to end. Now the best way to improve your writing and strengthen your skills is to complete several more pieces.

This step will help you gain a wealth of writing experience — and build up a portfolio of finished pieces in the process.

YOUR ASSIGNMENT

If you're primarily a prose writer, repeat Steps 7-21 five times or more, to create at least five more finished pieces. If you're primarily a poet, repeat these steps as often as necessary to finish a dozen new short poems. And if you work more or less equally in prose and poetry, finish three new prose pieces and six new works of poetry.

Follow the same process as before: Begin by selecting a focus; write a first draft; revise your work; edit and proofread; get feedback from one or more critics; and revise, edit and proofread further. Repeat any of these steps as often as necessary.

Throughout your work on this step, continue to use your writer's notebook, both as a place to record strong images and ideas and as a source of material for each new poem, essay or story.

In each of these pieces, feel free to work with whatever genres, forms, approaches, subjects, themes, styles or ideas you wish. The choice is entirely yours; write whatever moves you.

Because no one will see your work until you're ready to show it to them, you have enormous freedom — the freedom to try virtually anything you please. Don't be afraid to experiment, or to try out a variety of subjects and/or genres. If something works, great; if it doesn't, simply rewrite that piece or section.

If, on the other hand, you prefer to stick with one genre, a single subject or both, that's fine, too. Concentrating your energies in a single direction can result in rapid, focused growth. If you write six science fiction stories in a row, for example, you'll have probably become a much better science fiction writer (and a better writer in general) than you were when you finished your first science fiction piece. By becoming a specialist, you can focus your development as a writer and carve out a niche for yourself and your work.

If you choose to specialize, however, make sure that you don't write the same piece over and over. It's easy for beginning writers to come to the same conclusion, make the same point, evoke the same range of emotions, or follow the same general plot in each new piece they write. Once you've written three pieces, compare them carefully to make sure you're breaking new ground in each one, not simply writing variations on a single theme. If you do repeat yourself, make a point of deliberately doing something quite different in each new piece you write.

It's important that you get good feedback from at least one other person on each of your stories, essays or poems. Keep in mind that as you change genres, topics or approaches, you may need to change critics as well. Someone who was your ideal critic for one piece (e.g., a political essay) may not be the right person to critique the next (e.g., a poem or a horror tale). Before you get feedback from anyone, even someone who's been an excellent critic of your work in the past, make sure they're interested in and sympathetic to the type of piece you've written.

You don't have to write these new pieces one at a time. If you like, you can work on two or more at once. With experience, and perhaps some trial and error, you'll learn how many pieces you can work on at a time while still effectively focusing your energy.

Continue to keep in mind that nothing you write is ever bad or wrong but, at worst, simply unfinished. You can always revise whatever you've written. If part or all of your piece doesn't do what you want it to, keep working on it until you get it right.

Sometimes, though, a piece simply may not come together for you. This happens to experienced as well as not-so-experienced writers. If it happens to you—or if you simply get fed up with your piece or lose interest in it — stop working on it. You can always come back to it in the future. In the meantime, tell yourself that you've gotten some valuable writing experience, and begin a different story, poem or essay. (Incidentally, the unfinished piece doesn't count as one of the five you'll need to complete to accomplish this step.)

Don't forget to save everything you write — finished or unfinished, successful or unsuccessful. Even an unsuccessful fragment may prove useful sometime in the future.

Each time you finish a new piece, pat yourself on the back. And once you've completed this step, reward yourself with something you enjoy — a movie, dinner out, an afternoon off, etc. At the same time, remind yourself of this: You've already become a practicing writer. Not only that, but with each new essay, story or poem that you complete, you become an increasingly experienced one as well.

Read the Work of Good Writers

I s it essential to read widely in order to write well? No, not really. But is it helpful? Yes, enormously.

Reading the work of writers you enjoy will provide you with specific, concrete examples of how good writing works. You'll have a chance to see a variety of approaches and techniques in action, and you'll be able to analyze how these move and influence readers. At the same time, you'll get to enjoy and appreciate what you read.

Actually, reading almost anything — even best-sellers, popular magazines and newspapers — can benefit your writing. *People* magazine, *Ellery Queen's Mystery Magazine*, and *The Wall Street Journal* aren't likely to publish much great literature, but most of what they publish is competently written and, thus, potentially instructive.

You may think that I'm going to trot out a list of specific books for you to read, but I'm not. In fact, I'm not sure it's fair to. If I've learned anything from more than thirty years of reading and more than fifteen of teaching, it's that people's tastes vary widely. Clearly, there is no one book or body of literature that you *must* read to become a good writer. Furthermore, no one piece of writing has ever pleased everyone, or ever will. When it comes to both reading and writing, there is room not only for differences in taste, but for outright disagreement.

The guiding principle behind this book is to write what moves, intrigues or fascinates you. Now let me give you some related advice: Read what moves, intrigues or fascinates you. It doesn't matter what literature professors or book critics or anybody else thinks. You're the one who's reading, and who knows better than you what appeals to you and what doesn't?

Here's another piece of advice: Whatever genre you're working in (or plan to work in), read lots of material in that genre. There's no better way to see what's already been done, what works, what doesn't work, what's being published, and what approaches and techniques are available to you. If you write (or are interested in writing) fantasy stories, read contemporary and traditional fantasy. If you want to write travel articles and children's stories, look at some current travel magazines and some recent kids' books and periodicals. If you're thinking about writing a sonnet, look at what's been written before and what's being published now. (Yes, new sonnets — including some excellent ones — are being published today in very respectable magazines.)

Should you read any or all of the literary classics? If you like; it's entirely up to you. Reading literature that has lasted for decades or centuries can certainly help your writing, but it's by no means a necessity. (William Shakespeare managed to write quite well without having first read Mark Twain.) I suggest the following: Pick up some of the classic books and short pieces that look most promising to you — or that have been recommended to you by people whose opinions you value — and try them out. If you find yourself enjoying a certain literary work, wonderful. But if, after giving it a reasonable try, you're bored or turned off, put it aside and read something else. Don't expect to like (or dislike) any piece of writing just because of its reputation. Much of what's called great literature is seriously flawed; indeed, I haven't met anyone yet who genuinely enjoyed *all* of the literary classics.

How much reading should you do? It depends on how much time you have available. If possible, I suggest reading two books (or the equivalent in shorter work) per month.

YOUR ASSIGNMENT
This step contains five parts.

1. Set aside some regular time to read — ideally an hour a day or several hours a week. If this is too ambitious — and for most people, it is — two to three hours of scheduled time per week will do. It's important to specifically set aside this time, however — otherwise, it's likely to disappear in the flurry of daily obligations.

2. In your notebook, write a list of some things you'd like to read in the months to come. You don't need to read everything on this list, and you don't have to go through it in any kind of sequence. However, when you're not sure what to read next, simply pick some-

thing from this list. Add to the list regularly in the future as new items occur to you.

What should you include on this list? Anything you've ever wanted to read but haven't; anything that sounds intriguing or catches your eye; anything recommended to you by someone whose judgment you respect; and anything that seems potentially relevant to a writing project you're working on (or planning to work on). Be sure to focus at least half of your reading in the same genre(s) in which you work (or intend to work).

3. Spend some time browsing among the books and magazines at these four places: the largest library in your area (ideally, the main branch of a big-city library or the library of a major university); the biggest newsstand or magazine store near you; and the two largest bookstores you can easily get to. Bring your reading list with you. Wander among the shelves at your leisure, sampling whatever looks intriguing. Look at periodicals as well as books.

Do most of your browsing among the genres that most appeal to you, or that relate to the pieces you're writing (or planning to write). If you're interested in writing humor, look at humorous books and magazines; if you're at work on several feminist essays and short stories, peruse feminist literature and magazines such as *Ms.*

While it's okay to seek out specific titles, spend most of your time simply wandering, looking and sampling, without a specific goal or agenda.

Give yourself plenty of time—at least half an hour at the newsstand and no less than an hour in the library and each bookstore. Write down the titles of any interesting-looking items on your reading list, and buy or borrow some of the books and periodicals that intrigue you most.

4. Read some or all of the items you've acquired. If you find something particularly interesting, instructive or inspiring, make notes on it in your notebook—or photocopy and save the appropriate pages. If something you read provides inspiration for your writing, by all means use it—or write it down in your notebook for later use.

If you lose interest in something you're reading, there's no law that says you must finish it. Put it down and read something else.

5. Repeat parts two and three of this step at regular intervals—at least every three months, and every two if possible. Continue practicing this step indefinitely—not just for a few months, or a year, or until you finish this book, but for as long as you continue writing.

Reading should be an ongoing part of your growth and development as a writer.

However, don't let your reading cut into your writing time. If your time is tight, and you must make the difficult choice between reading and writing, choose writing 90 percent of the time. While reading and writing can reinforce and inspire one another, reading is never an adequate substitute for writing.

Furthermore, *never* read to avoid writing, or use reading as an excuse not to write. Reading should support your writing, not get in its way.

Reading can also take the form of listening. Writers in virtually all genres regularly give public readings of their work at colleges and universities, museums, art centers, writers' centers, bookstores, coffeehouses, bars, restaurants, community centers, and a variety of other public locations. These readings can give you an opportunity to sample other writers' work, as well as the chance to meet other writers. Many public readings are free, but some have an admission charge.

There's one other aspect of reading that's important to touch on, and that's reading books and magazines about writing.

This book you're reading now is intended to give you a solid start in writing stories, poems and/or essays—and to provide you with a thorough introduction to writing as an art, a craft and a process. However, if you'd like a wider or more advanced look at the act of writing, read one or more of the following:

Books:

1,818 Ways to Write Better & Get Published by Scott Edelstein (Writer's Digest Books). This is a good general introduction to many aspects of writing.

Writing Down the Bones (Shambhala) and *Wild Mind* (Bantam), both by Natalie Goldberg. These books focus on the writing process, the writer's attitude, and how writers perceive and transform reality.

Three Genres by Stephen Minot (Prentice-Hall). This is an excellent, if slightly academic, intermediate guide to writing fiction, poetry and drama.

On Writing Well by William Zinsser (HarperCollins). This is a very useful book on writing nonfiction of virtually every sort.

The Television Writer's Handbook (Barnes & Noble) and *The Screenwriter's Handbook* (Barnes & Noble), both by Constance Nash and Virginia Oakey. These are excellent guides to writing for Holly-wood.

The Indispensable Writer's Guide by Scott Edelstein (HarperCollins) and *This Business of Writing* by Gregg Levoy (Writer's Digest Books). These are two thorough, straightforward and helpful volumes on the business side of writing, and on building a writing career.

Magazines:

Three regularly published magazines offer a wide range of useful articles and columns on virtually every genre and aspect of writing: *Poets & Writers* (published bimonthly), *The Writer* (published monthly) and *Writer's Digest* (published monthly).

Discover What Inspires You

O ver the course of the first twenty-three steps you've gained a great deal of useful experience — experience in observing, reading, thinking, feeling, planning, outlining, writing, rewriting, editing and proofreading. Now is an excellent time to review this experience and see what guidance it can give you for your future writing.

In this step you'll review your goals, your reading interests, your notes, your finished pieces, your work habits, and your overall process for writing. In particular, you'll look at what most inspires you to write — and at what inspires you to write your best work.

YOUR ASSIGNMENT

Get comfortable in your primary work space. On your work surface in front of you, lay out the following items: your notebook; the final version of each of the pieces you've written so far; and your working notes for each of these pieces (from Step 7). If you like, also place your outlines, netlines and/or early drafts of these pieces nearby.

Directly in front of you, place a blank sheet of loose paper. Write "Sources of Inspiration" at the top of this sheet.

Begin by reviewing your writing goals in your notebook. How many of these have you met so far? Which are you well on your way to attaining? Which are you still some distance from reaching? Now that you have a good deal of writing experience behind you, are there any goals you wish to change? Are there new ones you'd like to add, or old ones you'd like to get rid of? How have your goals helped or hindered you? Has any goal gotten in your way — e.g., have you been too ambitious? How can your goals be changed so that they inspire and energize you as much as possible? Write down any helpful changes, additions or deletions on your "Sources of Inspiration" page.

Next, consider how and where you work. What about your work space(s) has been most helpful and inspiring? Least helpful? Most distracting or difficult? Which changes would you find most useful and inspiring? (Should you rearrange the furniture? Move your desk closer to the window? Get a space heater to take the chill off? Replace that ugly poster? Add a floor lamp? Disconnect the phone? Be firmer with your kids about not interrupting you?) On your "Sources of Inspiration" sheet, write down exactly what you can do to make your work space(s) as functional and supportive as possible.

If you write in more than one location, where have you done your best writing? Your most productive and efficient writing? Your poorest or least productive writing? Write down this information.

Now turn to your writing schedule. On what day of the week have you been most productive and efficient and/or done your best work? What time of day has worked best for you? Have you frequently found it difficult to write (or write well) at certain times? If the interval between your writing sessions sometimes differs (e.g., if you usually write on, say, Mondays, Thursdays and Fridays, as opposed to every day or each Thursday), what interval seems to precede your best or most productive writing? Again, jot down your answers for later reference.

Next, look at your writing habits. These might include a prewriting ritual, the background music you play as you write, the refreshments (or lack of them) you keep nearby, how you dress for writing, and so on. Have all of these been as helpful and effective as you want them to be? What can be changed, added or done away with to better support your writing? Write down whatever useful ideas you have.

Consider what you've read over the past months. Which books and short pieces provided you with the most inspiration and material for your own writing? Which writers? Which genres? Make a note to focus at least some of your future reading in these directions.

Then turn your thoughts to the people who have given you feedback on your work. Which of them have been the most helpful, insightful and/or inspiring? Whose comments have been the least helpful, and perhaps even harmful or discouraging? Write down which critics to seek out and which ones to avoid in the future.

The last part of this step requires your full, thoughtful and careful attention, so plan to take your time. If you need more than one session to complete it, that's fine.

What you'll do is go through most or all of what you've written so far: your entire notebook, your finished pieces, and, if you like, your drafts, outlines and netlines.

Begin by paging through your notebook, reading each entry carefully. Look at your list of things that move you; your collected thoughts and observations; your notes from your dreams and daydreams; the connections and patterns you discovered in Step 7; your working notes for pieces, also from Step 7; and anything else you've chosen to include in your notebook.

Read through each of your finished pieces carefully, one by one. If you like, look at your early drafts and/or outlines or netlines as well. Read this material in chronological order, from the earliest piece to the most recent one.

As you read through this material, consider these questions:

- Of all the images, ideas, concerns, emotions, themes, subjects, people and settings that appear frequently in your work, which are the most vivid, powerful or effective? Which hadn't you previously been aware of? Which surprise you?
- Do any particular words or phrases show up repeatedly?
- What genres, approaches and/or styles do you work with most often? Which most excite you? Which have resulted in the most moving and successful pieces?
- What other connections or recurring items do you see in your work that you may not have noticed before?

Write down your responses to these questions on your "Sources of Inspiration" sheet.

As you look through all of this material, new ideas, images, lines, plots or other useful items may emerge for you. Write these down as well.

When you've finished reviewing all of your material, take a short break. Then come back and look closely at your "Sources of Inspiration" page.

This page will serve as a blueprint for your future writing. It will provide you with suggestions for enhancing your writing circumstances and your writing process; with a list of the key elements that mean the most to you; and with the techniques, approaches and forms that will make your writing more vivid and powerful.

Post this "Sources of Inspiration" sheet in a prominent place in your primary work space — or tape it to the cover of your notebook. It will serve as a master plan for your writing in the months to come, offering you continuing guidance.

As the final part of this step, look back again — briefly, this time — at the most recent piece you've completed, then at the first finished piece you wrote, and then at the initial entries in your writer's notebook. Compare these items for a few minutes, recalling what you thought and felt as you wrote each one.

Then take a few moments more to appreciate how far you've come and how much you've grown as a writer since you first began reading this book.

Become Familiar With Common Forms and Terms

T his step will familiarize you with the major literary genres and forms, as well as with most of the specialized terms used frequently by writers, editors, critics, writing teachers and other literary people. While you don't need an intimate knowledge of everything in this step, it *is* important to read through it, so that you can have a sense of what your colleagues are talking (and sometimes writing) about.

YOUR ASSIGNMENT

Carefully read through all of the definitions and descriptions in this step. Make notes on anything that seems important to you.

It isn't necessary to memorize any of the material in this step. However, keep this book handy so that you can consult it and review any descriptions or definitions whenever you need to.

If you have not written poetry and have no plans to write any, you may skip over the sections titled "Poetic Terms" and "Poetic Forms."

Major Forms of Writing

Every piece of writing falls into one (or more) of three basic categories: prose, poetry and scripts. *Prose* is written in paragraphs, *poetry* (or *verse*) in lines and stanzas, and *scripts* in dialogue and stage directions (descriptions of settings, situations and actions to be performed by characters).

Any piece of written work can also be classified as a form of creative, personal, business, technical, professional or scholarly writing. *Creative writing* is writing in any genre whose primary aim is to evoke emotions. The other types of writing are all forms of prose that are used primarily to convey information and ideas.

Ninety-nine percent of all writing done in English, and at least 95 percent of all writing published in any language, is prose. There are two general types of prose: fiction and nonfiction.

There are no hard-and-fast definitions of either of these two literary forms. In general, however, *fiction* is prose that concerns itself with emotional truths rather than with literal ones; *nonfiction* is prose that recounts (or is substantially based on) real events. Nonfiction is written and published far more frequently than fiction.

The primary nonfiction form is the *essay*. Forms of essays include biography, autobiography, memoir and family history; news stories, features, editorials and opinion pieces; reports of all types; personal, philosophical and political pieces; reviews; and scholarly and professional articles. Virtually every nonfiction book can be considered either a single lengthy essay or a collection of shorter essays.

The major forms of fiction are:

The *novel*. A lengthy work of fiction, usually at least 40,000 words long. A novel normally has one central *plot* and one or more *subplots* (secondary plots), which build to a climax and resolution near the book's conclusion.

The *novella* (or *short novel*). A midlength piece of fiction, typically between 20,000 and 40,000 words. Structurally, novellas closely resemble novels, and they usually employ many of the same literary devices. However, novellas tend to contain fewer characters, a simpler central plot and fewer (or no) subplots.

The *short story*. A brief piece of fiction usually of less than 10,000 words. Typically, a short story is based on a single plot or event and involves no more than a handful of characters. (Some stories have only one or two characters.) In its most popular and traditional form, a short story begins with one basic conflict; this conflict worsens, creating a tension that builds more or less steadily to a climax; a significant change then occurs in one or more characters and/or in their circumstances; and a resolution (not necessarily a happy or satisfactory one, however) is reached. Over the past several decades, a variety of alternative structures and approaches for the short story have been developed; today, both traditional and nontraditional short stories are frequently published side by side.

The *novelette*. A term sometimes used for short stories longer than 10,000 words.

The *short-short story*. A very brief story (typically of 1,000 words or less), often with a surprising or ironic twist at the end. The term is sometimes used to refer to *any* story briefer than 1,500-2,000 words.

The boundaries between fiction and nonfiction are—and have always been—rather hazy. Humorous essays, for example, are usually considered nonfiction, even though they may be anything but factual. Some "short stories" are, in fact, accounts of actual events, but they are published as fiction because their emotional content rather than their literal truth stands out as most important. (Furthermore, as strange as it sounds, it's sometimes easier to publish certain types of essays as short stories than it is to publish them as nonfiction.)

Other literary forms that straddle the line between fiction and nonfiction include:

The *vignette* (or *slice of life*, or *study*). A brief fiction or nonfiction piece that focuses on and describes a single occurrence, place or person. Most vignettes have no climax or resolution.

The *docunovel*. These books, such as Truman Capote's *In Cold Blood*, Tom Wolfe's *The Electric Kool-Aid Acid Test*, and Norman Mailer's *The Executioner's Song*, document real occurrences in novelistic form, and employ many of the techniques of fiction. Although docunovels are usually based on thorough research, they are not usually 100 percent accurate; in these works, absolute precision sometimes takes a back seat to plotting and literary technique.

Creative prose. (1) Any nonfiction work that employs many of the techniques of fiction, or that is intended primarily to move rather than simply inform the reader—e.g., Maxine Hong Kingston's "No Name Woman," Dylan Thomas's "A Child's Christmas in Wales," or any of the docunovels noted above. The term *creative nonfiction* is synonymous with this definition. (2) A piece of fiction written as if it were an essay—e.g., Jorge Luis Borges's "Pierre Menard, Author of Don Quixote" or Woody Allen's "Lovborg's Women Considered."

Of the major forms of writing, poetry offers the widest array of specific, well-established approaches. I'll describe a number of these in "Forms of Poetry," which begins on page 125.

Most verse written and published today does not have regular rhyme or meter. However, these devices are anything but dead or outmoded; in fact, a significant portion of poetry being published today makes use of regular meter, rhyme or both. (Most good poems that do not use recurring meter or rhyme do, however, make use of a variety of other poetic techniques.) Both rhymed and unrhymed poetry have been around for many centuries, and it's highly unlikely that either will ever go out of style.

The *prose poem* is a crossbreed of poetry and prose. A prose poem can be defined in two ways: (1) a very short piece of fiction or nonfiction, usually fewer than 500 words (and almost always fewer than 1,000), which employs many of the techniques of poetry, especially imagery and sound devices; (2) A poem in which the traditional lines and stanzas are replaced with one or more paragraphs.

There are essentially two types of scripts, one traditional, the other modern:

The *play*. A script written to be performed by one or more actors before a live audience. A *full-length play* consists of two or three acts, and normally takes one to three hours to perform. A *one-act play* is a brief play of (usually) forty minutes or less.

The *electronic script*. A script, of any length, written for radio, television, film, filmstrip, audio or audiovisual production. Although there are occasional live performances of such scripts on radio or television, most electronic scripts are written to be recorded, edited and played back later.

At one of the points where poetry, prose and scripts all merge we find the *song*, which is a work of prose or poetry (usually poetry) intended to be sung according to a specific musical score. Although many songs rhyme, they don't have to. There are of course hundreds of different types of songs, from opera to rock 'n' roll to gospel to Tibetan Buddhist chants to advertising jingles.

It's quite possible for a piece to fall into two or more of these genres at once. For example, a poem can tell a fictional story, or a play can be written in verse.

General Writing Terms

The list that follows defines many of the commonly used words and phrases that pertain to writing, editing and publishing. Some of these terms have been used and/or defined previously in this book.

Acronym. A word (or a nonword read as a word) made up of the initial letters of other words—e.g., *NASA* (National Aeronautics and Space Administration) or *snafu* (situation normal—all fouled up).

Active voice (or **active language**). Writing that shows people, groups, organizations and creatures doing things, as opposed to events simply occurring. The following sentences are in the active voice: *I ate lunch. Audrey delivered the package to Eduardo.* Compare these sentences with those in the **passive voice** (or **passive language**): *Lunch was consumed. A package was delivered to Eduardo by Audrey.* Or, worse, *Delivery of the package was accomplished.*

Advance. Money paid to a writer by a book publisher in advance of publication in exchange for the right to publish the writer's work. Like a salesperson's draw against future commissions, an advance is applied against a book's future earnings.

Allegory. A tale in which the characters—and often the setting, central images and/or plot as well—are not meant to be taken literally, but are symbolic of specific things, ideas, institutions or events. George Orwell's *Animal Farm* is a modern allegory.

Ambiguity. Anything that can be understood or taken in more than one way. Used intentionally and carefully, ambiguity can add depth and power to your writing. Confusing or unintentional ambiguity, however, can have precisely the opposite effect.

Automatic writing (or **free writing**). Writing down whatever comes into your head, without pausing, editing, or (in some cases) following common rules of English usage.

Bibliography. A list of sources used in the writing of an essay. This list is included for readers' reference at the end of the piece.

Book proposal (sometimes called **portion and outline**). A package presented to book publishers for the purpose of securing a publication contract for a book that has not yet been completed. Typically, a book proposal consists of one to several finished chapters; a detailed plot synopsis (for fiction) or outline (for nonfiction) of the entire book; a brief overview of the book; an "about the author" page; and, if appropriate, an introduction and/or a table of contents. For details on book proposals, see *How to Write a Book Proposal* by Michael Larsen (Writer's Digest Books).

Cadence. The rhythmic flow of language in a literary work, particularly a poem. The term refers primarily to the pattern of accented and unaccented syllables, but also to other sound devices, and to changes in pitch and volume.

cf. An abbreviation meaning *compare with* or *compare to*.

Character. Any person who appears in a literary work. An animal playing a significant role, as in Jack London's *The Call of the Wild* or the Curious George stories, is also considered a character. Fairies, elves, trolls, robots, etc. can be characters as well. **Characterization** refers to the creation, use and development of characters.

Cliché. Any trite or overused idea (*war is hell*), phrase (*it's raining* *cats and dogs*) or image (*the pipe-smoking professor in a jacket with leather elbows*). Clichés are instantly recognizable but carry little power or meaning.

Climax. The point of greatest conflict or tension in a literary work. A resolution or change of some sort usually occurs simultaneously, or soon afterward. Some literary works have one or more secondary climaxes in addition to a primary one.

Context. Situation.

Denouement. The final resolution or sorting out of events in a literary work.

Development. The buildup of plot, characters, images, ideas and other elements.

Dialect. A specific variant of a language that has its own vocabulary, intonations, pronunciations and/or grammar. In various dialects, *Nuts! What rotten weather!* becomes *Uff da! What ishy weather!* or *This weather sucks, man,* or *Oy, weather like this I've never seen.*

Dialogue (also spelled dialog). Usually, any verbal exchange between people or characters. Sometimes used to refer to any words spoken by a character, even one person talking to themselves.

Diction. Proper word choice, apart from considerations of grammar. *I opened the bag containing the lunch belonging to me* is grammatically correct, but has very poor diction: It's clumsy, it's not standard American English, and it just plain sounds wrong.

Draft. A version of a piece of writing composed more or less from beginning to end. A **first draft** is the first such version; a **second draft** is the second version; and so on. A **final draft** is a finished piece.

e.g. For example.

Ellipsis points. Three or four periods in a row. Used to indicate a pause, a gap (usually in time), or an omission of words. When used at the beginning or end of a passage, ellipsis points indicate a fading in or a trailing off. Normally you would use three ellipsis points; use four dots, however, to indicate the omission of the end of a sentence, the omission of the beginning of the following sentence, or the omission of one or more entire sentences.

Epiphany. A moment of realization, awakening or sudden insight. An epiphany can occur for a character, the reader or both.

First person. Writing that has *I* or *we* as its subject. Examples: *I'm hungry. I don't want to go to Chelsea.*

Flashback. A scene that transports the reader out of the main flow of events to an incident that took place previously.

Focus. A widely used but potentially misleading term that can mean point of view, theme or emphasis, depending on its context. When it's used in relation to your work, it's best to ask to have the word defined.

Foreshadowing. The use of imagery, dialogue, or some other literary device to hint (often subliminally) at future plot developments.

Free writing. See **automatic writing.**

Genre. A literary form — e.g., fiction or poetry. The term can also be used to refer to forms within forms, such as short stories or novels, or to specialized fields, such as science fiction and Westerns.

Gerund. A verb transformed into a noun by adding *ing* to it, as in *drinking, thinking* or *having.*

Homonym. A word that sounds exactly like another word but that has a different meaning, and usually a different spelling as well. Some examples: *stair* and *stare; shoe* and *shoo; gross* (noun), *gross* (verb), and *gross* (adjective).

Hyperbole. Deliberate — and usually extreme — exaggeration used to add emphasis. Hyperbole frequently takes the form of a **metaphor** or **simile.** It is often intentionally humorous, and is rarely meant to be taken literally.

Ibid. Used in footnotes, endnotes and lists of references, this simply means *from the source most recently cited.* It's normally underlined or italicized and followed by a page number.

Idiom. Any expression that's widely used but not literally true, logical or sensible. Examples: *We danced up a storm. I feel like you're feeding me lies. I think I'll take a rain check on that.*

i.e. That is.

Image. Any sensory impression or set of such impressions. An image can engage any of the senses, or any combination of two or more. **Imagery** is the use of images.

Infinitive. Any verb with the word *to* before it — e.g., *to laugh, to eat, to remember,* etc.

Irony. An outcome, result or occurrence that is exactly the opposite of what was planned, hoped for or expected — e.g., a city dweller moves to the country to be alone, only to find himself visited incessantly by neighbors who feel lonely and isolated. The term also refers to a figure of speech in which the intended meaning is exactly (and deliberately) the opposite of its literal meaning — e.g., saying to a runner as she zooms past, "Good morning, Pokey."

Lyrical. Musical-sounding. Not to be confused with a **lyric poem** (see page 125), or with **lyrics**, which are the words to a song.

Metaphor. A literary device that compares or relates one person, thing or idea with another, either directly or by implication, through the use of an image. Metaphors are of course not literally true. Example: *Max was a demon on the trading floor.* Compare with **simile.** See also **trope.**

Mixed metaphor. (1) A metaphor that confuses or inappropriately combines two images; (2) Two metaphors carelessly thrown together. Examples: *Sour grapes are not my cup of tea; I was just shooting off my mouth at the messenger.*

Monologue. A speech, of any length, made by one person or character in a literary work. An **internal monologue** (sometimes called an **interior monologue**) is the presentation of one person's extended thoughts or deliberations.

Mood. The overall feeling or atmosphere created by a passage, scene, stanza or entire piece. Compare with **tone.**

Narrator. The voice or character in a literary work who relates what occurs. In Bill McKibben's *The Age of Missing Information*, McKibben himself is the narrator; in other works, such as Mark Twain's "The Notorious Jumping Frog of Calaveras County," the narrator *purports* to be the author but is in fact a character of the author's creation. A **disembodied narrator** is a narrator who has no specific persona; most newspaper articles have such a narrator, as do some poems and fiction pieces, such as Shirley Jackson's "The Lottery." An **omniscient narrator** is a disembodied narrator who has superhuman powers of perception. An omniscient narrator might, for example, describe several characters' innermost thoughts, or relate events that none of the characters could possibly be aware of. Some literary works, such as William Faulkner's *As I Lay Dying*, have several narrators; others, such as Woody Allen's "The Gossage-Verdebedian Papers" (which is composed entirely of letters between two increasingly antagonistic chess players), have no narrator at all. **Narration** is the relating of events by a narrator. A **narrative** is a stretch of narration, or a piece composed entirely of narration.

Non sequitur. (1) A phrase that's meaningless or irrelevant — e.g., *Nixon's the one*; (2) Any inference or conclusion that doesn't logically follow from its premises, as in *It may be winter, but I'm going* *to buy a briefcase.* Non sequiturs (especially political slogans) often sound more meaningful than they are.

Obscure. (1) Unclear, vague or ambiguous; (2) Unknown or virtually unknown.

¶. A symbol for the word *paragraph.* Inserted between two sentences, it indicates where a new paragraph should begin. *No ¶* at the beginning of a paragraph means *merge this paragraph with the previous one.*

Pacing (also called **pace** or **rate of revelation**). The speed at which events take place in a literary work. If a great deal happens in a few lines or paragraphs, the pacing is rapid; if there is little movement of events for several pages, the pace is relatively slow.

Paraphrase. To restate something in different words, often in condensed form. Used as a noun, a paraphrase is any passage that provides such a restatement.

Parody. A form of humor (and sometimes ridicule) in which a person, event, institution or thing (e.g., a magazine, or a particular writer's style) is imitated and exaggerated to the point of absurdity.

Parts of speech. The eight basic types of words: nouns (*ghost, nose*), pronouns (*she, them*), verbs (*grow, write, be*), adjectives (*heavy, bright, redundant, sneaky*), adverbs (*slowly, happily*), prepositions (*near, around*), conjunctions (*and, nevertheless*) and interjections (*wow, oops*).

Phonics (or **sonics**). (1) The use of rhyme, meter and other sound devices, usually in a poem; (2) How a poem (or other literary work) sounds.

Plot. The sequence of events in a literary work. Some works have a central plot and one or more **subplots**, or secondary sequences of events; other pieces have no plots or subplots at all.

Portion and outline. See **book proposal.**

Point of view. See **viewpoint.**

Protagonist. The central character of a literary work. Some pieces have more than a single protagonist (John Steinbeck's *Cannery Row*); others have no protagonist at all (Theodore Roethke's poem "Root Cellar").

Pseudonym (or **pen name**). A false name used by an author as a byline.

Re. Regarding.

Redundant. Unnecessarily repetitious, as in *unusual and unique* or *"I'm furious!" he shouted angrily.*

Rhetoric. The art and strategy of using language effectively, especially to convince or persuade people.

Rhythm. The ebb and flow of sound in a literary work, particularly its pattern of stressed and unstressed syllables. The term is sometimes used to refer to variations in pacing.

Royalty. The percentage of a book's retail or wholesale price (or the portion of a play's ticket price) that goes to the author. A **royalty statement** is a periodic report of these earnings.

Satire. A type of humor that pokes fun at a person, idea, thing or institution, usually by exaggerating one or more of its qualities.

Scene. A clearly defined portion of a literary work that recounts a single event or sequence of events. Usually a scene takes place in a single location and/or is written from a single point of view. Compare with **setting**.

Second person. Writing that has *you* as its subject. Examples: *You don't understand. When you see it for yourself, you'll change your mind.*

Setting. (1) Location; (2) A description or set of images that establishes a location and its overall atmosphere.

Sic. When quoting someone else, add *sic* in brackets (or, if you have no brackets, in parentheses) immediately following any error of fact, grammar, spelling, etc., to indicate that the error is theirs, not yours. Example: *In response, Mr. Flammarion smiled and said, "Hey, that's small tomatoes [sic], honey."*

Simile. A comparison of one person, thing, image or idea with another, through the use of *like* or *as*. Examples: *After three months of dieting, Sue was thin as a reed. They stared at each other, like two cats about to fight, or mate, or both.* See also **trope**.

Soliloquy. A monologue spoken by a character in a play, sometimes directly to the audience.

Sonics. See **phonics**.

Stet. A proofreading and editing term that means *as it was*. When you've changed something in your writing, and you realize later that the way you previously had it works better, simply write *stet* above your change to indicate that the change should be ignored.

Stereotype. An overly simple, one-dimensional representation of a person, place, group or institution.

Stream of consciousness. A writing technique that presents the thoughts of a character as they occur. Stream of consciousness may use standard English or a modified form of English intended to mimic actual thought. Not to be confused with **automatic writing.**

Subplot. See **plot.**

Subsidiary rights. The right to publish, produce, record, perform, or otherwise display or distribute a literary work once it has been initially published or performed.

Symbol. A literary device in which a person, object, image or event is used to evoke a meaning other than (or in addition to) itself. The use of symbols is called **symbolism.**

Synecdoche. A figure of speech in which a single part or element is used to represent the whole—e.g., when a king is referred to as *the crown.* In another form of synecdoche, a single member of a group is used to represent that entire group. In the sentence *There are fewer June Cleavers today than there have ever been since 1955,* June Cleaver serves as a synecdoche for happy, submissive, middle-class housewives. See also **trope.**

Synopsis. A compressed narrative description of a literary work. In a work of fiction, the term **plot synopsis** is more common. Synopses may be written in either the first or third person, and in either the past or present tense. In book publishing, a synopsis is often (incorrectly) called an **outline.**

Syntax. Sentence structure.

Theme. Any important concern, idea, topic, point or statement in a piece of writing.

Third person. Writing that has *he, she, it, they* or a noun as its subject. Examples: *She'll never believe you. It's a lie! The Democratic Party has controlled Congress for years.*

Tone. How a piece of writing (or an individual section or passage) sounds. Compare this with **mood.** The tone and mood of a literary work can sometimes differ dramatically; e.g., the tone of much of Edward Gorey's work is quite grim, yet the overall mood is usually lighthearted and funny.

Trope. Any word or expression used in a sense other than what is commonly intended. Metaphor, irony and synecdoche are all forms of tropes.

Usage. Rules and standards for language, including grammar, punctuation, syntax, diction and spelling.

Viewpoint (or **point of view**). The perspective through which events and images are related and/or viewed. A literary work can be written from the viewpoint of one of its characters, its author, a bogus author (i.e., someone who claims to be the author but is in fact a creation of the author), or a disembodied or omniscient narrator (see **narrator**). A single literary work may also make use of two or more different viewpoints — usually but not necessarily two or more of its characters. The following sentence, about a character named Henry, is written in the third person but is nevertheless from Henry's viewpoint: *Henry stopped, knowing he was trapped, and looked frantically in both directions. He had to find a way out.*

Voice. The tone and manner in which a narrator writes and/or speaks.

Poetic Terms

A complete introduction to poetic terminology would require a full book. Indeed, there already exists an excellent volume on the subject, Paul Fussell's *Poetic Meter and Poetic Form* (Random House). A good (but shorter) introduction to poetic terms and conventions also appears in the "Prosody" section of *The Norton Anthology of Poetry* (Norton). *Prosody*, by the way, is the study of patterns of sound, such as meter and rhyme.

Below is a brief and, of necessity, somewhat less than complete introduction to the most important poetic terms and concepts:

Stanzas are groups of lines separated by a single line of blank vertical space. A stanza can be any length, from one line to an entire poem. The end of each line is called a *line break*; the end of each stanza is a *stanza break*. Each line break or stanza break creates a visual pause, but not necessarily an aural one (i.e., one you'd hear if the poem were read aloud, or that you hear mentally when you read the poem silently).

A two-line stanza is known as a *couplet*; a three-line stanza, a *tercet* or *triplet*; a four-line stanza, a *quatrain*; a five-line stanza, a *cinquain* or *quintet*; a six-line stanza, a *sextet* or *sestet*; a seven-line stanza, a *septet*; and an eight-line stanza, an *octave*. (Longer stanzas have no formal names.)

Any emphasis on a single syllable is called an *accent* or *stress*. (Such a syllable is thus said to be *accented* or *stressed*.) The pattern of stressed and unstressed syllables within each line of poetry is called *metrics* or *meter*; any group of two or three syllables is known as a *poetic foot*. The metrics of any given line of poetry (except lines containing only a single syllable) are made up of one or more poetic feet.

There are seven poetic feet. Each represents a different pattern of stressed and/or unstressed syllables:

Iamb (or *iambic foot*): An unstressed syllable followed by a stressed one, as in *hello, Japan, arrange, today* or *the roof*.

Trochee (or *trochaic foot*): A stressed syllable followed by an unstressed one, as in *baby, sled dog, common* or *backward*.

Dactyl (or *dactylic foot*): A stressed syllable followed by two unstressed ones, as in *natural, basketball, superglue* or *other one*.

Anapest (or *anapestic foot*): Two unstressed syllables followed by a single stressed one, as in *understand, jubilee, in a sense* or *overwhelm*.

Amphibrach (or *amphibrachic foot*): Three syllables — the first unstressed, the second stressed, the third unstressed. Examples: *condition, arrival, my darling, the plumber*.

Spondee (or *spondaic foot*): Two stressed syllables in a row, as in *M.D., heartbeat, head nurse* or *stay calm*.

Pyrrhic (or *pyrrhic foot*): Two unstressed syllables in a row. Examples: *by the, in a, so he*.

Note that in some cases a poetic foot can include two or even three words. In other cases, a single word may be made up of two or more poetic feet; the word *paramecium*, for example, is made up of one pyrrhic and one dactyl. (It's of course possible for certain words to be pronounced or metrically analyzed in more than one way.)

A poetic foot that ends on an accent has *rising meter*; one that ends on an unaccented syllable has *falling meter*.

A line containing only one poetic foot is a line of *monometer*. If a line consists entirely of the same foot repeated twice, it is a line of *dimeter*; a line repeating the same foot three times (and containing no other syllables) is a line of *trimeter*; four times, *tetrameter*; five times, *pentameter*; six times, *hexameter*; and seven times, *heptameter*.

The meter (if any) of a poem reflects the type and number of poetic feet in each line. If each line of a poem contains four dactyls (e.g., *Under the willows we settled our differences*), that poem is written in *dactylic tetrameter*. If the first line of a poem contains three iambs (e.g., *I never thought to look*), that line is composed in *iambic trimeter*. If a line includes two or more kinds of poetic feet, it is written in *mixed meter*.

Sprung rhythm is a variation of traditional poetic feet in which each foot consists of a single accented syllable followed by any number of unaccented ones. When read aloud, however — or when heard mentally during silent reading—each foot takes up the same interval of time. The following line uses a sprung version of iambic tetrameter: *He said I was a fool for showing my rage.*

To *scan* a poem is to identify the type and number of poetic feet in each line. *Scansion* is how a poem scans.

Rhyme is, of course, a repetition of the same sound—either the same vowel sound (as in *do* and *crew*), or the same combination of a vowel sound and a consonant sound (as in *map* and *trap*, or *messy* and *Bessie*, or *tureen* and *the screen*).

The pattern of rhyme in a poem is called its *rhyme scheme*. Specific rhyme schemes are represented by the first few letters of the alphabet. For example, in a quatrain in which lines one and four rhyme with one another, and lines two and three rhyme with each other (but not with lines one and four), the rhyme scheme would be written *ABBA*. If lines one and two were to rhyme with each other, and three and four with one another, the rhyme scheme would be *AABB*; and if all four lines were to rhyme with one another, the rhyme scheme would be *AAAA*.

Other common—and useful—poetic terms include:

Alliteration. The identical initial sound in two or more words, as in *bat* and *barbecue*, or *crisp* and *crass*. Words do not need to be immediately sequential to be alliterative.

Assonance. The repetition of the same vowel sound, as in *better yet*, *black hat* or *under the bundle*. Assonance can appear in any syllable(s).

Blank verse. Unrhyming iambic pentameter. Not to be confused with **free verse.**

Canto. A section of a poem, usually numbered.

Consonance. Repetition of the same consonant sound in any syllable or syllables, as in *stepped stealthily, renowned name* or *gathering throng*. This last example includes two instances of consonance.

Free verse. Poetry written without regular rhyme or meter. Good free verse nevertheless makes use of a variety of other poetic techniques; it may also use rhyme and/or meter in an irregular fashion. Do not confuse with **automatic writing** (see page 115) or **blank verse.**

Onomatopoeia. Words and phrases that sound much like what they mean, as in *crunch, snap, grunt, goop* and *slush*.

Refrain. A recurring line, phrase, group of lines or stanza in a poem or song.

Forms of Poetry

Poetry does not need to conform to a preset structure; indeed, most of what is written and published today does not. However, several forms of verse follow clear (and often complex) rules. These include:

Ballad. A poem or song that tells a story. Ballads are usually made up of four-line stanzas that rhyme *ABCB* or *ABAB*. Compare with **ballade.**

Ballade. A poem of three eight-line stanzas, each of which rhymes *ABABBCBC*, followed by a single four-line stanza (called an **envoy**) which rhymes *BCBC*. Don't confuse this with a **ballad.**

Haiku. A traditional Japanese and Chinese form of verse that lends itself surprisingly well to the English language. A haiku consists of a single stanza of three brief lines. Lines one and three are five syllables each; line two is seven syllables. Traditionally, a haiku does not rhyme, and contains (or focuses on) a single vivid or surprising image, often involving nature. Although American haiku writers have often strayed from the naturalistic tradition, they have not modified the five/seven/five structure.

Lyric. A short poem expressing a single emotion, narrated by a single speaker. Not to be confused with lyrics, which are the words to a song. Compare with **lyrical** (see page 118).

Rondel. A poem of fourteen lines that rhymes *ABBAABABAB-BAAB.* Line one is identical to lines seven and thirteen; line two is identical to lines eight and fourteen.

Sestina. A rigidly structured form of verse containing six six-line stanzas and one final three-line stanza (or **envoy**). Stanzas two through five all conform to the following pattern: The final word in line one is the same as the final word in line six *of the previous stanza*; the last word in line two repeats the last word in line one of the previous stanza; the final word in line three repeats the final word in line five of the prior stanza; the last word in the fourth line is the same as the last word in the previous stanza's second line; in line five, the last word repeats the last word of the prior stanza's fourth line; and the final word in line six is the same as the last word in the third line of the previous stanza. The concluding three-line stanza contains all six of these repeated words. A sestina normally does not rhyme.

Sonnet. A fourteen-line poem, in iambic pentameter, that follows a rhyme scheme such as *ABBAABBACDECDE, ABBAABBACDC-DCD, ABABCDCDEFEFGG* or *ABABBCBCCDCDEE*. A sonnet normally contains one to four stanzas. The Italian (or Petrarchan) sonnet, the most interesting and dynamic sonnet form, sets up a tension or problem in the first eight lines. A major shift appears after line eight, and the final six lines of the poem provide an answer, resolution or response to those first eight lines.

Villanelle. A complex form of verse made up of six stanzas. The first five stanzas are each composed of three lines that rhyme *ABA*; the sixth stanza consists of four lines, and usually rhymes *ABAA*. Lines one, six, twelve and eighteen are identical; line three is distinctly different from line one, but identical with lines nine, fifteen and nineteen. Two key words traditionally appear throughout the poem; each is used separately and changes its resonance or meaning each time it appears. A tension builds throughout the poem and is resolved in the final line, in which the two key words are at last used together.

It is quite permissible to vary any of these forms to suit your purposes. For example, you might write a poem that's similar to a sonnet but that contains eighteen lines instead of fourteen, or that employs hexameter instead of pentameter.

All of the forms described above continue to be practiced and published today, though in some cases (e.g., the rondel) not widely.

At this stage you've accumulated a good deal of writing experience; you've begun a self-designed reading program; you've become acquainted with a variety of important terms and forms; you've built up a storehouse of material to work with in the future; and you've assembled a collection of completed pieces that all bear your byline.

Now you're ready to get your best work into the hands of readers. So turn to Part Five, and I'll show you how to start submitting your pieces to editors for publication.

Getting Published

Prepare a Manuscript for Submission to Editors

S o far, you've been writing for three important reasons: to please yourself, to grow steadily more skilled as a writer, and to create the best poems, stories and/or essays that you can. Now I'd like to suggest a fourth reason: to share your insights, observations and talents with an audience. The single best way to do this, of course, is to publish your work.

I don't mean to suggest that you *must* publish (or try to publish) what you've written. Publishing your work is always an option, never an obligation. Indeed, there are other excellent ways to share your work with others: give a public reading; pass out copies to your friends; or read it aloud to your family, and perhaps discuss it afterward. And remember, you needn't show your work to anyone until you're ready — or ever, if that's what you prefer. The choice is entirely yours. Nevertheless, as a writer, it's important that you at least know *how* to get your best work published.

You need to be selective, of course. Don't rush to publish everything you write. When you feel a piece is finished, ask yourself, "Is this piece good enough to be published, or is it really just a useful exercise?" If it's an exercise, file it away. But if you feel that readers will find it moving and rewarding, don't let modesty or fear hold you back. Get that piece into the hands of editors.

Keep in mind, however, that the publishing world is not always reasonable, honest or fair. A great deal of good writing gets turned down by editors for arbitrary, silly and even downright stupid reasons. Mark Twain's hyperbole about publishers — *there are two types of publishers: crooks and incompetents* — still rings true (as hyperbole) today. Nevertheless, a well-written poem, story or essay is always far more likely to be published than one that has obvious weaknesses.

For more details on getting published and building a writing career, see my book *The Indispensable Writer's Guide* (HarperCollins).

YOUR ASSIGNMENT

If you're primarily a prose writer, look through the six finished pieces you've written so far, and ask yourself which are strong enough to merit publication. Then select from this group the one piece of prose that you believe is the best you've written.

If you're primarily a poet, pick your five best short poems; or, if some of your poems are more than two or three pages long, select eight to twelve pages of your best work. Submit all of these poems together, in a single batch. (If your best work is a single poem longer than five pages, submit it alone.)

If you genuinely feel that you haven't yet written a publishable story or essay, or a sufficient amount of publishable poetry, don't go any further with this step right now. Instead, continue to focus your attention on writing as well as you can, and create several more new pieces by repeating Steps 7-21. Then, sometime in the future, when you feel you've written material that's truly worth publishing, return to this step. (However, don't let fear, resistance or modesty steer you away from this step forever.)

It's essential that each manuscript you submit be prepared according to the accepted standards of the publishing industry. These standards are arbitrary, of course, but they help make the process of publishing a little easier and more consistent for everyone. Properly preparing a manuscript is like dressing up for a job interview; it makes an appropriate first impression, and it conveys the message that you know what's expected of you.

Prepare your manuscript according to the following guidelines:

As noted earlier, use plain, white, medium-weight (16 or 20 lb.) 8½-by-11-inch paper. Use paper without lines, holes or rounded corners. Standard photocopying or computer paper works well and is available for two to four dollars a ream (500 sheets). Use only one side of each page; leave the other side blank.

Type your manuscript on a letter-quality typewriter, word processor or computer printer. A dot-matrix printer is not okay; laser or ink-jet printing is necessary. Use only a dark black ribbon or black ink. Pick a typeface that's clear and easy to read, such as Ariel, Courier, Helvetica, Times Roman or Prestige; avoid ornate typefaces such as Script, Modern or Impact.

Use one of the following type sizes: pica, elite, ten point, twelve point, ten pitch or twelve pitch. One exception: You may, if you wish, use a larger size for your title—but only on your first page.

Set margins of about an inch on all four sides. Leave the right margin unjustified (uneven).

Each page beyond the first should have what is called a *page heading* at the top. Each heading includes the page number and some key words that quickly identify your piece—e.g., its title, a significant portion of the title (such as *Mockingbird* for *To Kill a Mockingbird*), your full or last name, or some reasonable combination. Page headings should appear in the same location on each page—either flush left, flush right or centered. Begin your text three or four lines below each page heading. (Note: The first page of each manuscript should not have a page heading or page number.)

Things not to add to your manuscript include: your social security number (your editor will ask for it if they need it); the rights you wish to sell (these are always negotiable); and a copyright notice (such a notice isn't necessary or useful until the piece is published).

Type or print out your manuscript as neatly as possible, so that it looks clean and attractive and is easy to read. If you need to make small changes, do so neatly in black pen. Better yet, use correction tape (thin strips of sticky white tape); cover the passage you wish to change with this tape, type the new passage directly on the tape, and photocopy the page. Or, if you prefer, retype the appropriate passage on a separate page; then cut it out, tape it over the old text with transparent tape, and use a photocopier to produce a corrected, clean-looking page. (If you have a word processor or computer, of course, simply make the corrections on the screen and print the entire page again.)

Do not staple your manuscript; use a large paper clip—or, for manuscripts of more than a dozen pages, a butterfly clamp (a large paper clip shaped vaguely like a butterfly). If you have printed your manuscript on continuous-feed paper, remove the side strips and separate the pages.

It's often useful (and sometimes a necessity) to have your piece(s) also available on a computer disk. Ideally, your work should be saved in Microsoft Word, on a 3½-inch floppy disk. Both IBM and Mac disks are normally acceptable. If you do not have Microsoft Word, and cannot translate your piece into that program with your word processing software, simply save your piece as an ASCII or text file. (Saving a piece in ASCII gets rid of all underlining, boldface and italics, but retains everything else.) If your manuscript is prose, mention in your accompanying letter that a disk version of your piece is available on request; if your submission is poetry, don't mention the disk at all. (I know this sounds strange, but it's the way of the publishing world.)

Special Instructions for Prose Manuscripts

Use the upper-left-hand corner of page one to provide editors with the following personal information, all of which should be typed single-spaced, flush left:

Line 1: Your name (not your pen name, if you use one);

Line 2: Your street address or post office box;

Line 3: Your city, state or province, and zip or postal code;

Line 4: Your telephone number(s). If you have both work and home telephones, include both, and indicate which is which. If you have a fax number, include this on a fifth line; if you have an e-mail address, put this on line six.

In the upper-right-hand corner of your first page, opposite your name, flush right, type "About ____ words"; fill in the blank with an appropriate rounded number. If your piece is 4,000 words or shorter, round the word count to the nearest 100 words; if it's 4,000 to 10,000 words, round it to the nearest 500 words; and if it's longer still, round it to the nearest 1,000 words.

In the exact center of this first page, type your title, either in all capital letters or in both capital and lowercase letters. Drop down two lines, then type your byline (e.g., "by Scott Edelstein"). If you are using a pen name, include it here.

Drop down four more lines and begin typing the text of your piece. This text should be double-spaced from beginning to end.

If you have written the text for a children's book (but not if you've written a short piece that you're submitting to a children's magazine), also prepare a cover page and a presentation folder. The cover page will be identical to the first page of your manuscript, except that below your byline the page should be left entirely blank. This cover page is "page zero"; the page that follows is page one. Then place

SAMPLE PAGES OF A PROSE MANUSCRIPT

Scott Edelstein   About 2,800 words
4445 Vincent Avenue South
Minneapolis, MN 55410
612-928-1922
612-928-3756, fax
CommConSE@aol.com

YOUR TITLE GOES HERE
by Scott Edelstein

This is the accepted format for most prose manuscripts. Note that, except where otherwise indicated, all text is double-spaced.

Follow this template unless you are writing an essay intended for an academic or scholarly journal, in which case do the following things differently.

First, create and add a cover page. This will have your title and byline in the center. About three inches below your byline, type your name, address, phone number(s), fax number (if any) and e-mail address (if any). These items should be centered, and each should appear on a separate line (with your address taking up two lines). Single space all of these items. Your cover page will have no header, footer or page number.

Your next page will be numbered page one, and will look exactly like page two of this sample prose manuscript, except that your piece will begin three or four double-spaced lines down the page. Subsequent pages will be identical to the sample of the following page.

Edelstein/2

This is the form to use for subsequent pages of any prose manuscript, including one intended for a scholarly or academic journal. There should be a page number and a header in the upper right corner of each page. This should include either your last name, the title of the piece, or a key word or phrase from the title.

If you need to begin a new section, you may simply skip a line, like so:

Another option is to add a line of asterisks, which I'll do at the end of the following paragraph. To add emphasis, simply *italicize* or <u>underline</u> the appropriate words or put them in **bold**. (But pick a single option and stick with it throughout your piece.)

Unless the piece has been previously published, don't include a copyright notice or the words "all rights reserved"; these are unnecessary and look amateurish. Also, don't include your social security number (you'll be asked for it at the appropriate time) or the rights you wish to sell (those will depend on where and in what formats the publication is distributed).

     *   *   *   *   *

It's fine to send editors clear photocopies, but make sure they are in good condition; shabby, dog-eared manuscripts announce to editors, "I've been rejected repeatedly."

Your manuscript should be as clean and error-free as possible. If you need to make a correction, it's best to print a new page rather than write in the correction by hand.

Your font may be 10, 12 or 14 point; 12 is most common. Experiment to learn what fonts are clear, attractive and easy to read. (Some fonts look tiny in 10 point, others look just fine.) Avoid fancy typefaces such as Script, Mistral or Modern; keep your manuscript looking clear and simple. Don't gussy it up with borders, clip art, dingbats, your photo or illustrations (unless they naturally accompany your piece).

your entire manuscript in the right-hand pocket of a two-pocket stiff-paper folder (the kind without either a gusset or fasteners). Type all of the information from your cover page on two to three blank labels, and affix these to the front cover of the folder. (For complete details on preparing and submitting a book manuscript, see *The Writer's Digest Guide to Manuscript Formats* by Dian Dincin Buchman and Seli Groves (Writer's Digest Books) and/or my book *The Indispensable Writer's Guide.*)

Special Guidelines for Poetry Manuscripts

Each poem, no matter how short, should be typed on a separate page and considered a separate manuscript. Longer poems may of course run more than one page.

With the exception of the upper-right-hand corner of the first page, each manuscript should be either single-spaced (double-spaced between stanzas) or 1½-spaced (triple- or 2½-spaced between stanzas).

In the upper-left- or the upper-right-hand corner of the first page, type the following information:

Line 1: Your name (not your pen name, if you wish to use one);

Line 2: Your street address or post office box;

Line 3: Your city, state or province, and zip or postal code.

If your manuscript is single-spaced, use single-spacing for this information; if your poem is 1½-spaced, use either single-spacing or 1½-spacing. If you place this information in the upper-left-hand corner, type it flush left against the left-hand margin; if you put it in the upper-right-hand corner, type it flush left against an imaginary margin about three inches from the right edge of the page.

Drop down four to six lines. Type the title of your poem in all capitals, flush left. Do *not* add a byline. Then drop down another three to four lines and begin your poem.

Do not include your telephone number(s) or fax number on your manuscript. (You may include these numbers in your accompanying letter, however.) If you wish your piece published under a pen name, do not use it or mention it. After your poem has been accepted for publication, call or write the editor and ask them to publish it under your pen name. This sounds strange, I know, but it's how things are done with poetry.

Clip all of your poems together into one batch with a single paper clip or butterfly clamp.

You now have a carefully written, well-prepared, neat-looking manuscript ready to be sent out to editors. Your main concern now is which editors are most likely to appreciate and publish your writing. In the next step, you'll learn how to discover for yourself which editors and publications will be your best bets.

SAMPLE PAGES OF A POETRY MANUSCRIPT

Harriet Martinez Gold
566 Winsbury Avenue
Washington, DC 20009
202-555-5969

AS YOU CAN SEE

The format for a poetry manuscript
Is quite different from one for prose.

Your poem should be either single-spaced
(And double-spaced between stanzas)
Or one-and-a-half-spaced, with two and a half
Or three spaces between stanzas.

You may either type your poem flush against
The left-hand margin of the page or establish
A separate left margin for your text that
Centers the poem on the page, as I've done here.

If your poem continues onto the next page,
Simply place a header and a page number
In the upper right corner of the page, as in the prose
Manuscript sample on the previous page.

In the case of an overlong line, you can indicate
That the same line continues by indenting
        several spaces, as I've done here.

If the poem employs visual effects, such as
the unusual
                placement of
                        words and lines,

        then feel free   to amend   this form as necessary.

As You Can See/2

Subsequent pages of a poetry manuscript
Should look like this. In general, try
To *not* break a stanza at the bottom of a page,
But continue it on the next page. Do, however,
Avoid printing the last line of a stanza as the
First line of a page—and try not to make the first

     Line of a stanza the last line of a page. (One-line
     Stanzas are the exception, however.)

Research Potential Markets for Your Work

E ach piece of writing has its own unique audience. Readers who will be moved by your poem about your brother's death are not necessarily the same people who will appreciate your short story about the battle of Appomattox. Doctors, parents, teenagers and Catholic priests might all be interested in reading an essay on birth control, but each group will want a different approach and perspective.

Each publication has its own unique audience, too—as well as its own slant, its own approach and its own agenda. *Science News* will not print a murder mystery or an article on how to buy stocks, no matter how well written either piece may be. And although *Ms.*, *Cosmopolitan* and *Ladies' Home Journal* are all women's magazines, only *Ladies' Home Journal* would publish "The World's Best Christmas Cookie Recipes," and only *Ms.* would publish an article on women in Somalia.

What does all this mean for you? Simply this: Getting published isn't just a matter of writing well. For each story, poem or essay that you hope to publish, you must locate those publications that print the type of material you've written, and that reach the same readers your piece seeks to reach. Thus it's essential that you do some careful market research to determine which publications (or *markets*) are right for your work.

The only truly effective way to do this is to examine a wide array of publications, one at a time. There are no short-cuts. You may, if you like, read through the market listings (brief descriptions of which types of writing various publications look for) in writers' periodicals, and in reference books such as *Writer's Market*. However, many of these listings are incomplete, misleading or out of date. These resources *can* help you establish an initial pool of promising-sounding publications; but you must then look through an issue or two of each one to really get a feel for what it publishes.

Most of the pieces that you write will be appropriate for more than one type of market. For example, a short story about two women who raced a dogsled across Minnesota might be published in a literary magazine, a general-interest magazine (e.g., *Harper's*), a women's magazine, a sports journal, a large newspaper's Sunday supplement, an outdoor publication, or a magazine that focuses on Minnesota or the Upper Midwest. An essay on a professional tennis player's breast cancer might be appropriate for a health magazine, a women's publication, a tennis or sports magazine, or the health and lifestyle pages of many newspapers.

YOUR ASSIGNMENT

Begin by writing a list of those publications that you think might be interested in your manuscript. If you like, use writers' magazines, newsletters and/or reference books (e.g., *Writer's Market*) to come up with ideas. If you have some doubts about certain publications, write them down anyway; you'll have your chance to check out each one thoroughly later in this step.

Visit a large newsstand or bookstore—one with the widest selection of magazines and newspapers that you can find. If there is no such store near you, it's worth making a trip to the nearest city to find one. Bring pens, paper, and your list of possible markets with you.

Browse at length among the various titles. Take your time; five extra minutes of research now can save you an hour of wasted effort later. Spend at least forty-five minutes looking around—longer, if you need to.

If a publication looks interesting, scan its table of contents and at least one or two of the pieces in it. Ask yourself these questions:

- Who does this publication try to reach?
- What slant, focus or perspective does it have?
- What themes, subjects and genres appear in it?
- How long are the pieces that it publishes? How long is the shortest piece in it? The longest?

Whenever a publication strikes you as an appropriate place to publish your work, write down its title, its editorial address (which may differ from its subscription address), its telephone number, and the name of the proper editor to approach. (I'll explain how to pick the right editor shortly.) In magazines and newsletters, you'll find all of this information on the contents page, or within four pages before or after it. In newspapers, this information normally appears on one of the editorial pages, which are usually near the rear of the first or second section.

If you need to look at a publication in more detail, either purchase it (it's a tax-deductible business expense) or make a note to look at it more carefully when you visit a good library.

And it's to a large library — the larger, the better — that you'll proceed next. This should be the main public library of a large city, the main library of a large university, or both. (If your work is appropriate for publication in literary magazines, it's a good idea to visit both.) The library will carry a wide range of publications that the newsstand does not — and vice versa.

Follow the same procedure that you went through in the newsstand or bookstore. Focus your attention only on current and recent issues; anything older than six months won't give you much of a sense of what that publication publishes *now*. Again, take your time; spend a couple of hours if you need to.

If you can't find a publication that you're looking for, ask a librarian to order the two most recent issues for you through interlibrary loan. Or, if you prefer, get the publication's address and telephone number from a reference librarian, and order a copy of the most recent issue directly from the publisher. Make your request in writing, and enclose a check for the cover price plus one dollar for postage. Another option: Call the publisher, explain that you're a writer interested in submitting some of your work, and ask for a copy of the most recent issue. Some publishers will send you a copy at no charge; at worst, you'll be asked to mail a written request and a check.

Continue your market research — visiting more libraries and/or stores if necessary — until you've drawn up a list of at least five publications that you feel will be interested in your work.

One important but often overlooked part of market research is getting the names of the right editors to approach. Locating the right editor is essential; if you send your work to the wrong person, or simply to "Editor" or "Fiction Editor," chances are good that it will be placed in what's called the *slush pile* — the group of manuscripts earmarked to receive the least serious and most cursory consideration. Here are some useful guidelines:

For Magazines and Newsletters

As you examine the list of editors and other staff members near the front of the publication, look for an appropriate department editor (e.g., the editor for travel, sports, fiction, poetry, etc.). Send your work to this person unless the publication has a very large circulation (e.g., if it's a magazine such as *Playboy*, *Mademoiselle*, etc.)—in which case write to the appropriate assistant or associate department editor, if one is listed.

If editors are not assigned to specific departments or genres, send your work to the editor or editor-in-chief (the titles are synonymous); if no such title is listed, send your submission to the person holding the position of publisher. One exception: In the case of large-circulation magazines such as *Harper's* or *The Atlantic*, step down a notch; write instead to an assistant or associate editor (or, if no such title is listed, a senior or managing editor).

For Newspapers

In the case of large- and medium-size papers, send your work to the appropriate department or section editor. This person's name should appear on one of the editorial pages—or, in some cases, on the first page of the appropriate section. Smaller papers—such as arts and entertainment papers, suburban papers, neighborhood papers, and other newspapers published no more than twice a week—may not have department editors at all. In this case, send your submission to the feature editor. If there's no feature editor, send it to the editor or editor-in-chief; and if no such position is listed, send your work to the publisher.

If two or more editors of a publication share the same job title, pick one at random.

You can always, of course, simply call up any publication and say, "Can you tell me who's your current _____ editor?" (Some of the larger magazines may refuse to give out this information, however.) Another option is to check the most recent edition of the reference works *The Working Press of the Nation* or *Bacon's Guide*, available in some large libraries. These contain good lists of editors for most newspapers and magazines published in North America.

If you've finished a book manuscript, you'll need to conduct your market research differently. Go straight to a good library and ask for the most recent Spring and Fall Announcements issues of the magazines *Publishers Weekly* and *Library Journal*; if you've written a children's book, get the most recent Children's Books for Spring and Children's Books for Fall issues instead. Read these issues carefully, including the ads; they'll give you a good sense of what many presses are publishing. I also recommend that you order current catalogs (usually available free) from those presses that look most promising. For publishers' addresses and telephone numbers, and the names of their editors, consult the annual reference books *Writer's Guide to Book Editors, Publishers, and Literary Agents* and *Literary Market Place*, available in many large- and medium-size libraries.

Here are a few other general tips on doing market research for your writing:

• It's not hard to get published in most big-city newspapers. But the larger a circulation a magazine has, or the more well known it is, the tougher it is to get published in it. As a result, magazines such as *The Atlantic, The Saturday Evening Post, Redbook, Cosmopolitan, Playboy* and *The Paris Review* rarely publish work by new writers. For this reason, I suggest sending your submissions primarily to local, regional, special-interest (e.g., *Outside, Dog Fancy, Relix, Ski, Alfred Hitchcock Mystery Magazine*, etc.), and other small and mid-size publications. After you've published four or five pieces in these publications, your chances of getting published in big-name magazines will go up considerably.

• Perhaps you've seen display ads in writers' publications and the Yellow Pages that begin "Get Published," "Authors Wanted," or "To the Author in Search of a Publisher." These ads are for *vanity presses*—book publishers that print virtually anything that comes their way, so long as the author is willing to pay a fee for the privilege. Vanity presses produce decent-looking books, but bookstores rarely order them (would *you* order books from a publisher that prints everything it receives?). This means that almost every vanity press book is a financial flop for the author. Some variations on vanity publishing include: literary contests that exist primarily to make a substantial profit from contestants' entry fees; magazines, literary agents and book publishers that charge writers a fee to have their work read and considered; "co-publishing" arrangements in which authors share publication costs with a publisher; and poetry anthologies that accept for publication virtually any poem, so long as the author orders and pays for a copy of the anthology in advance—usually at a cost of twenty-five to fifty dollars. Do not go along with any of these schemes. You may, however, consider self-publishing, which is a more honest—and usually more potentially lucrative—arrangement.

• Avoid on-line marketing services that store literary works in a database for instant access by publishers. Few publishers and editors actually use these services.

At this point you've got a manuscript ready to submit, a willingness (if not an eagerness) to send it out, and a list of people and publications to submit it to. You're ready to pack up your work and send it on its way. In the next step you'll learn how to present your work to editors most professionally and effectively.

Submit a Manuscript for Publication

I n this step you'll bring together everything you've learned from all of the previous steps. You'll assemble five complete submission packages, and you'll put these in the mail to editors at five publications. Along the way, you'll also write some more.

Each submission package should contain either a single work of prose (of any length), or five to seven short poems totaling no more than twelve pages. If you have longer poems, you may submit fewer than five, for a total of up to twelve pages. And you may submit a single poem by itself in either of two situations: if the poem is longer than five pages, or if you are sending it to a special-interest publication (e.g., if you're sending a poem about sailing to a sailing magazine).

An essential part of any submission package is a *cover letter* — a brief letter introducing your work (and, if appropriate, yourself). Writing a good cover letter usually isn't difficult; it's largely a matter of following a standard form and a few simple rules.

Your cover letter should be brief and to the point — normally no more than three or four short paragraphs on a single page. The writing should be clear, concise and businesslike; a cover letter is a communication between professionals, not a sales pitch or advertisement. Prepare each cover letter in standard business letter form, using black ink, single spacing, a standard font and type size, and a letter-quality printer, typewriter or word processor.

The first paragraph of your cover letter should describe your submission briefly, in a single phrase or sentence — e.g., *I'm pleased to send you "The Painted Moon," a short story set in contemporary Zimbabwe*, or *I've enclosed a copy of "Borrowing 101," a parents' guide to the Department of Education's new higher education loans*, or *I wanted you to have a chance to see my most recent feature, "Santa on a Surf-*

board," a factual but not terribly reverent look at Christmas in Australia, or *Enclosed are several of my newest poems. . . .*

If your submission is a piece of nonfiction intended primarily to help or instruct readers, you may, if you wish, explain why your piece is useful or important — but don't take more than a few sentences to do it. For example: *Last summer, Congress made some sweeping changes in how — and how much — it will allow parents to borrow for their kids' college educations. On the surface, the new regulations appear to be more liberal, permitting more borrowing and a more flexible payback period. But these policies could saddle the next generation of college students with burdensome debts that they'll still be paying back as they approach middle age. The enclosed article, "Borrowing 101," takes a hard-nosed look at the U.S. Department of Education's new regulations, and focuses on the specific ways in which these changes will help and hinder college students.*

Your next paragraph should — again, briefly — present a small amount of information about you. This information must either establish you as an experienced and serious writer, relate your background or experience to your submission in some way, or both. For instance: *These poems are based on the three years I spent as a child in an Algiers orphanage, which bears little relation to the orphanages here in North America.* Or, *I've written fiction for the past two years and have enjoyed your magazine for well over a decade.* Or, *I've published short pieces in two area newspapers, and have an essay forthcoming in the magazine* Pig Iron. You must tell the truth, of course — though there's nothing wrong with putting the most positive spin on it. (The "pieces in two area newspapers," for example, might be brief book reviews in two neighborhood publications). Don't mention anything that will sound trivial or irrelevant, like your honorable mention in the local Kiwanis Club's writing competition. If you have nothing relevant to add about yourself — and this is often the case with newer writers — you may omit this paragraph entirely.

Your final paragraph is your chance to add a few details pertaining to your submission. First, let the editor know that you're enclosing a self-addressed stamped envelope (or SASE). If you can provide a computer file of your piece on a floppy disk, say so, but don't include a disk with your submission. (And if your submission is poetry, don't even mention a disk or computer file at all.) Conclude this paragraph with a friendly closing statement of no longer than one sentence.

Type or print out a separate letter for each editor; never use a photocopied form letter. Each cover letter should be addressed to the appropriate editor by name, not merely by title (e.g., write to "Nathan Maxwell, Feature Editor," not just to "Feature Editor"). If you're not sure whether the person you're writing to is a man or a woman—e.g., if they're named Chris, Lynn, Marion, etc.—begin your letter with the full name (*Dear Chris Fussell* or *Dear Lynn Marting*).

YOUR ASSIGNMENT

Begin by writing a strong cover letter according to the guidelines above. Then assemble five complete, professional-looking submission packages, one for each of the five editors and publications you selected in the previous step. Follow these specifications:

Make five clear, clean photocopies of your manuscript; keep the original in your files, and submit the photocopies. (Or, if you own a word processor or computer, you may make six originals—one for you, and five for editors.) Clip your manuscript and your cover letter together in the upper-left-hand corner with a paper clip or butterfly clamp. The cover letter should be on top, as if it were "page zero" of your manuscript.

Behind the last page of your manuscript, inside the paper clip, slip your self-addressed stamped envelope. You have two options here. If you'd like your work returned if it's not accepted for publication, the SASE should be large enough to accommodate the manuscript, and there should be enough first-class postage on it to cover the manuscript's return. If you prefer, however, you may instead include a #10 business envelope with a single first-class stamp on it, and in the final paragraph of your cover letter say something like this: *I've enclosed a stamped business envelope. If you're not interested in publishing the enclosed material, simply let me know via letter, and recycle or destroy the manuscript.*

If you send your work to a publication in another country, *don't* enclose an SASE. Instead, enclose an unstamped, self-addressed business envelope and a single International Reply Coupon. (IRCs are redeemable for postage in any country in the world and are available at most large post offices.) In the final paragraph of your cover letter, explain that you're enclosing an IRC; ask the editor to respond by letter, and to recycle your manuscript if it's not accepted for publication.

Slip the whole works—manuscript, cover letter and SASE—into

23019 Santa Barbara Drive
Evanston, IL 60202
312-224-9971

December 9, 1993

Jerry Wexler
Travel Editor, *Imaginary Life*
34 Spring Street, Suite 406
St. Paul, MN 55101

Dear Mr. Wexler:

Chicago's O'Hare Airport is the busiest in North America and the fourth busiest in the world. Unfortunately, for most travelers, O'Hare is about as familiar as the ruins of Machu Picchu and as easy to deal with as the programming instructions for their VCRs. Indeed, most adult Americans live in secret (if minor) dread of either hearing or having to say the words, "I'm stuck at O'Hare."

The enclosed travel feature, "Surviving O'Hare," is intended to provide relief. It's a user-friendly, hands-on guide to arriving at, leaving from, getting around, eating and drinking in, and generally taming the beast known as O'Hare.

I've been a frequent business traveler — usually in and out of O'Hare — for the past seven years, and have made negotiating the airport something of a personal mission for the last five.

The usual SASE is enclosed. If you have any questions, or if you'd like to see a disk copy of this article — or if you're ever stuck at O'Hare and need some sage advice — give me a call.

Regards,

Alice M. Valentino

3444 Klein St., #12
Milwaukee, WI 53202
414-988-2009 (w)
414-290-0117 (h)
414-290-0128 (FAX)

November 20, 1993

Tracy Macaulay
Assistant Editor, *Sample Magazine*
288 Conklin Ave.
Fort Smith, AR 72903

Dear Tracy Macauley:

I'm pleased to send you my newest short story, "Opening Lines," which I hope you'll want to use in an upcoming issue. The story concerns the first meeting of two cousins raised in very different subcultures; it is set in rural Arkansas, a location that I know has long been of interest to *Sample*.

I've been writing fiction seriously for well over a year, and have been a serious reader of *Sample* for at least a decade.

A computer file of "Opening Lines" is available on a floppy disk at your request. For now, I'll enclose a stamped business-size envelope; if you choose not to publish this story, simply let me know by letter, and recycle or dispose of the manuscript copy. If you have any questions, feel free to call. Enjoy the upcoming holiday.

Sincerely,

Carla McNaughton

Enc.:
"Opening Lines"
SASE

an envelope large enough to easily accommodate it all. Generally, you should mail your submission, flat and unfolded, in a 9-by-12-inch or 10-by-13-inch envelope. However, if your manuscript and cover letter together total six pages or less, you may fold the material in thirds and mail it in a regular business-size envelope.

Neatly type all names, addresses and return addresses on both your mailing envelope and your SASE. If you use manila envelopes, type this information on mailing labels; affix these to the envelopes.

Mail your work via first class — or, if it exceeds ten ounces, either priority mail or UPS. You may use a courier service such as Federal Express, but this won't impress anyone. Don't submit manuscripts via fax or modem unless you have specifically been asked to do so. If you send your work outside the country, use air mail; the post office has special rates for manuscripts sent air mail to certain countries.

You do not need to copyright your work before submitting it (it is fully protected by copyright law from the moment of its creation), nor do you need to mail a copy to yourself to prove ownership.

When you've got five packages put together, weigh them, affix sufficient postage, and drop them in the mail.

The practice of sending the same piece to more than one publication at a time is known as making *simultaneous* or *multiple submissions*. Most professional writers follow this practice, which has become the norm in almost every area of publishing. However, there are a few exceptions to this rule. It is not considered kosher to send the same piece simultaneously to two or more newspapers that have significantly overlapping readerships (e.g., the *Minneapolis StarTribune* and the *St. Paul Pioneer Press*), or to two or more professional, technical or scholarly journals. If either of these conditions applies to you, alter the requirements of this step appropriately.

Once you've sent out your manuscript, don't wait expectantly by the telephone or mailbox. Get on with your life and your writing. Do, however, make a note on your calendar to follow up your submission if you haven't received a response within a reasonable amount of time. Wait ten weeks for a reply to any prose submission, fifteen for poetry (or for any submission to a literary magazine). In either case, make a brief, polite telephone call to the editor; if they ask for more time to consider your work, say, "No problem. I'd appreciate a response within a month, though." If, after twenty weeks have passed, you've still not gotten a yes or no, consider the submission lost, ignored or otherwise dead, and send your work to another editor.

If a publication decides to use your work, congratulations! If your work is rejected by all five editors, however, don't feel discouraged. Rejection is an occupational hazard for most writers. I still get rejected most of the time; in fact, much of what I publish gets rejected several times (sometimes *dozens* of times) before it finds a home. Shrug your shoulders and send out your manuscript to some other editors; if necessary, do additional market research first.

What if two (or more) editors want to publish the same piece? This is neither as likely nor as big a problem as it may seem. Once a piece has been accepted for publication, simply write a brief, businesslike note to each of the other editors who are considering your work. In the case of directly competing publications, explain that you've had the piece accepted elsewhere, and that you're therefore withdrawing it from their consideration. If you like, add a note to the effect that you hope to be able to send them a new submission shortly. (In the case of poetry, only withdraw the particular poems that have been accepted for publication; any others can remain as live submissions.) For publications that do not directly compete with the magazine, newspaper, newsletter or anthology that has accepted your work, use your letter to explain the situation, and emphasize that your piece has been accepted by a publication with a different audience. Let the editors know that your piece remains available for publication, but as a reprint rather than a previously unpublished work.

At this stage you've accumulated all the basic knowledge and experience you need. Your next step is to gain more experience and to apply your talent, effort, patience and persistence (both as a writer and as a marketer of your work) to establishing yourself as a professional. In Step 29, we'll take a look at what you can do to look, act and think like a pro — and be recognized and acknowledged as one.

Think and Act Like a Pro

Y ou've been a practicing writer for some time now. You've written a number of finished pieces, and you've begun to make connections with editors and to seek publication of your work. You've come a long way — especially if you were an absolute beginner when you began with Step 1.

But it's the policy of this book not to let you rest on your laurels for long — which means that you've got another task ahead of you: becoming a practicing *professional* writer.

According to one common definition, a professional writer is anyone who has had at least one piece accepted for publication by a respectable book, magazine, newspaper or newsletter publisher. But I know of people who have published widely and earned a considerable amount of money from their writing, but whose attitudes and actions are anything but professional.

What really makes someone a professional writer is their attitude, the way in which they approach the art, the craft and the business of writing. The real pro may or may not have published anything yet, but they bring commitment, energy, integrity and patience to their writing, as well as to their personal and professional dealings with others. It should come as no surprise that these are the writers most likely to be successful in the long run.

There's no simple set of instructions for becoming a full-fledged professional writer. It's a gradual and ongoing process. But if you do your best to follow the guidelines below, day by day, you'll slowly and steadily become more and more of a pro.

YOUR ASSIGNMENT

Below is a list of practices, principles and guidelines that most professional writers routinely follow. Read them carefully; if you like, post them prominently in your work space, or add them to your writer's notebook.

As you write and market your work, do your best to practice each of these principles. At first you may feel awkward or uncertain, and things may not always go as you would like them to. But as you write each new piece and gain more publishing experience, you'll gradually find yourself becoming more and more of a seasoned pro—one piece, interaction, submission, business deal or publication at a time.

- Keep your expectations reasonable—for yourself, for editors, and for other publishing people.
- Be straightforward and honest in all your business dealings.
- Be civil and businesslike at all times—in person, on the telephone and in letters—even if the individual you're dealing with is not.
- Don't be afraid to try new topics, genres, forms, approaches or markets. If a new or unusual (but worthwhile) opportunity presents itself, go for it.
- Be clear about what you want, need and expect.
- Don't expect editors and other publishing people to be perfect. *Do* expect them to treat you fairly, honestly and with respect.
- Live up to whatever commitments you make—and expect editors and publishers to do the same.
- Don't promise what you can't deliver, and never agree to any terms that you're unwilling or unable to fulfill.
- Expect—and, if necessary, insist on—reasonable fees, terms and deadlines.
- Stick up for what you feel is appropriate and fair. If necessary, insist on it. Don't let yourself be mistreated.
- If a problem arises, make it known to the appropriate person promptly and straightforwardly.
- When you make a mistake, miss a deadline or cause a problem, apologize promptly and do what you can to make amends.
- Be willing to make reasonable compromises—but refuse to make unreasonable ones.
- Use proper manuscript form for all submissions, and standard business letter form for all correspondence.
- Accompany all submissions with well-written cover letters.
- Properly cite your source whenever you use anyone else's words or ideas.

- Quote all sources as accurately as possible.
- Don't lie or twist the truth in any piece of writing intended to be factual. Be as accurate as you can.
- When doing research for a piece of writing, be as thorough, careful and detailed as necessary.
- Present your credentials truthfully and accurately, but in the most positive light.
- Meet or beat all deadlines.
- Use the telephone whenever it will be most efficient, convenient or effective. Otherwise, use the mail and/or a fax machine. Call collect only when you've been asked to call.
- Set up a workable filing system, so that you can easily save and retrieve important documents.
- Keep copies of all your professional correspondence — both what you write (including faxes) and what you receive.
- Keep at least one master copy (preferably two) of everything you write.
- If you have a computer or word processor, save every file in at least two locations (e.g., on two floppy disks, or on a floppy disk and a hard drive).
- Send out a manuscript to editors only when you genuinely feel it's in the best shape that you can get it and consider it worthy of publication.
- Do proper market research for any piece you plan to submit for publication. If necessary, do market research for each new piece you write.
- Follow up submissions that have not been responded to within ten weeks for prose, and within fifteen weeks for poetry and all submissions to literary magazines.
- Read every contract thoroughly, negotiate it carefully, and save it in an easily accessible spot.
- Always make a clear, unambiguous agreement — preferably a written one — to cover the publication of your work. If you make an oral agreement, jot down the terms as you talk; then promptly send your editor a letter or fax that details those terms. Add something like this: "This is my understanding of what we've agreed to; if your understanding is different, please let me know."
- Always try to be paid on the signing of your publication contract or on the acceptance of your finished manuscript. Avoid pay-

ment on publication if at all possible. (One compromise: Set the payment date for a specific number of days—e.g., thirty, sixty, etc.—beyond signing or acceptance. The sooner, the better, of course.)

- Never agree to any terms you find unacceptable. If a publisher isn't willing to negotiate a fair, reasonable deal, it's better to have no deal at all.
- Never threaten a lawsuit except as a next-to-last resort. (The final resort, of course, is actually suing.)
- Keep accurate records of all of your submissions, acceptances and publications. Keep these records together in a submissions book or special file.
- Keep an accurate, ongoing account of all your business expenses. (These are normally tax-deductible on your Schedule C. If you have little or no writing income, these deductions can usually be used to reduce your total income from other sources.)
- Never throw away anything you write.
- Never pay anyone to publish your work—unless you've become your own publisher and you've hired a printer.
- Be patient and persistent. The people who succeed in the writing business are those who keep at it for years, despite rejection and setbacks, and who think and plan in terms of decades.
- Write as well as you can at all times.

To stay sane, a writing professional needs to keep rejection in perspective. Here is some advice to keep in mind as you market your work:

- Virtually all writers have their work rejected sometimes, and most have it rejected frequently. Whether we like it or not, rejection is an inevitable part of being a professional writer.
- Never take rejection personally. Your *piece* is being rejected, not you. Any rejection reflects only on the work you've submitted, not on your overall ability or promise as a writer.
- A piece can be rejected for dozens of reasons, and most of these have nothing to do with the quality of the work itself. Publications change their focuses or policies; editors get fired; pieces scheduled for publication get pulled at the last minute when an extra full-page ad comes in; and so on and so on.
- What one editor despises, another may adore. I've had pieces

published that were previously rejected with rude, angry and insulting comments.

- Don't let rejection shake your faith in a piece, or in yourself. If you believe in something you've written, keep sending it out — dozens of times, if necessary — until it's accepted. It's not uncommon for something to be accepted for publication after twenty, fifty or even a hundred rejections.
- Take editors' comments in rejection letters with a large dose of salt. Editors are not always good critics, and their comments are often written hastily and without much thought.
- If an editor rejects your piece but says positive or encouraging things about it, send them something else. And if they tell you that your piece came close, consider rewriting it and sending them the rewrite.
- Never tell an editor in a cover letter that a piece has been rejected before.
- Never write or call editors to argue the merits of a piece they've rejected. Instead, use your energy to send the manuscript to several other publications.
- If a manuscript begins to look worn from being read and rejected, make a new copy.
- If an editor turns down a piece, then leaves their job, feel free to send the same piece to their successor. One writer I know sold a short story to a major magazine after it had been rejected twice by two of the editor's predecessors.
- If one department editor at a publication says no to your piece, it may make sense to send it to a different department editor at that same publication. For instance, if the lifestyle editor at the *Cleveland Plain Dealer* rejects your humorous essay on arguing with teenagers, try sending it to the editor of the paper's Sunday magazine.

Once you've become a working professional writer, your primary task is to keep growing. In the final step in this book, you'll look to the future and to your continued growth and success as a writer.

Build Your Writing Career — and Continue to Grow as a Writer

This final step builds on everything you've done so far, from jotting down ideas in your notebook to maintaining the highest standards of professionalism. It involves planning your future as a writer and working to steadily expand your range, your recognition, your amount of income and your impact on readers.

It's possible to complete this step in a cursory fashion over a period of a few months, at which point you'll have completed this book's entire program. But this step isn't meant to be finished and then forgotten. It's meant to be put into practice continuously, over and over, as you become ever more able and successful as a writer.

YOUR ASSIGNMENT

First, take an hour or two to look back at how and where you started as a writer, where you've been throughout your writing career, and where you are now. Review all the steps you took and all the progress you made along the way. Look back at the early entries in your notebook and the first one or two pieces that you completed; compare these to what you're writing now. Then compliment yourself on all that you've learned, all the skills that you've developed, and all the results you've achieved over the course of the first twenty-nine steps.

Now turn from the past to the future. In the months and years to come, you'll repeatedly draw from everything you've learned as you practiced the steps in this book. Whenever you feel the need or desire, return to any step that seems appropriate. Reread it and, if necessary, repeat the activity that the step requires.

To help support your continued growth as a writer, and the growth of your writing career, also do the following:

- Keep writing regularly, according to a supportive schedule. If possible, increase the time you spend writing.
- Continue to take time to observe, think and meditate — and to write down images, observations and ideas in your notebook.
- Review the material in your notebook on a regular basis, and use it to inform and generate new stories, poems and essays.
- Submit your work to editors regularly. Send each publishable piece to at least three editors at a time. Keep each manuscript in circulation until it sells.
- Work on longer and more ambitious pieces — perhaps even a book, or a stage play, or a television or film script.
- Keep reading the work of writers you admire. Watch how they do what they do, and learn from them.
- Attend public readings by writers whose work interests you — and, once you've got enough writing experience under your belt, contact the organizers of a reading series to see about giving a reading yourself.
- Find more people who can serve as useful critics for your work in progress.
- If the company and/or criticism of other writers is important to you, join a writers' critiquing group. If you can't find one that you like, start your own.
- Join the National Writers Union and/or one or more professional writers' organizations (Western Writers of America, the Society of Children's Book Writers, the Poetry Society of America, etc.).
- If you like, pitch some ideas for *assignments* to editors of magazines and/or newspapers. (Assignment ideas are usually pitched by letter, but if you've built up an ongoing relationship with an editor, feel free to use the telephone instead.) Under this arrangement, you sign a contract to write a specific piece by a mutually determined deadline for an agreed-upon fee. Once you have enough experience and publications behind you, some editors may start approaching *you* with assignment ideas.
- Consider other ways to build your writing career: Suggest a regular column to a magazine, newspaper, newsletter or syndicate; sell your services as a writer to businesses and nonprofits; apply for jobs as a salaried writer or editor; or come up with your own writing-related entrepreneurial venture.
- Have professional letterhead, envelopes and address labels

printed—or run them yourself on a laser or ink-jet printer. Your letterhead should be simple in design and should include only your name, address, telephone number(s), and a brief title or description, such as "Writer" or "Literary Services" or "Writing and Editing."

- Get some business cards. Keep these simple, like your letter-head.

- Buy and use some basic business gear: a daily planner or appointment book; a postage scale (for weighing outgoing packages); a telephone answering machine (preferably one that can record telephone conversations as they take place); and a briefcase. If you conduct in-person interviews for your writing, get a portable tape recorder.

- Once your writing career is going strong, make a long-term investment in some serious hardware: a fax machine, a computer and printer (and word processing software), and a modem, all of which have become virtual necessities for many writers.

- Above all, enjoy yourself.

Throughout this book, I've done my best to give you all the tools you need to start writing, keep writing, steadily improve your writing, publish your writing, and ultimately become a professional writer of the highest caliber. I'd be pleased to receive letters from people who have been helped by this book—especially those who have become professional writers as a result of following and practicing its thirty steps. I'm also happy to receive general comments, criticisms and suggestions for future editions. Write to me at 4445 Vincent Avenue South, Minneapolis, MN 55410.

I've enjoyed serving as a guide on your journey as a writer. May the remainder of this journey be a steady source of satisfaction and success for many years to come.

INDEX